It's not fair!
'It's not fair!' is Kitty's pla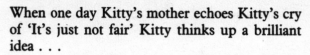
the shortest in her class?
her family take a joke? Wh
as late as the boy next door? Why don't holidays
last forever?

When one day Kitty's mother echoes Kitty's cry
of 'It's just not fair' Kitty thinks up a brilliant
idea . . .

But you promised!
This time Kitty's cry is 'But you promised!' as she
discovers that sometimes grown-ups make promises they can't keep – but then so do children!

Why not?
Kitty always used to say she didn't want to do
this or that. Then there was a change – she
wanted to DO things, but the grown-ups
wouldn't let her. Instead of saying 'I don't want
to!' she found herself asking 'Why not?' But the
reply she got was 'Because I say so'. But Kitty
finds her own way round every obstacle –
especially when she goes on holiday and wants
to go trick-or-treating . . .

Also by Bel Mooney

I don't want to!
I can't find it!
I know!

BEL MOONEY

HERE'S KITTY!

It's Not Fair!
But You Promised!
Why Not?

MAMMOTH

First published in Great Britain as three separate
volumes:

It's not fair!
First published 1989 by Methuen Children's Books Ltd
Published 1991 by Mammoth
Text copyright © 1989 Bel Mooney
Illustrations copyright © 1989 Margaret Chamberlain

But you promised!
First published 1990 by Methuen Children's Books Ltd
Published 1991 by Mammoth
Text copyright © 1990 Bel Mooney
Illustrations copyright © 1990 Margaret Chamberlain

Why not?
First published 1990 by Methuen Children's Books Ltd
Published 1992 by Mammoth
Text copyright © 1990 Bel Mooney
Illustrations copyright © 1990 Margaret Chamberlain

This omnibus edition published 1992 by Mammoth
an imprint of Reed Consumer Books Ltd
Michelin House, 81 Fulham Road, London SW3 6RB
and Auckland, Melbourne, Singapore and Toronto

ISBN 0 7497 1311 9

A CIP catalogue record for this title
is available from the British Library

Printed in Great Britain
by Cox & Wyman Ltd, Reading, Berkshire

Contents

It's not fair!

It's not fair!

...that I'm little

Kitty was the smallest girl in her class. Usually she did not care. She could swim well, and run as fast as most people – well, almost – and once came first in the egg and spoon race on Sports Day. So it did not matter – being small. That was what Kitty thought.

But one day something happened to make her change her mind. It was one of those days when nothing went right.

First of all, there was a new boy in Kitty's class. His name was Tom, and he was very, very tall. Kitty didn't like him very much, because he called her 'Shrimp'.

The whole class was working on a mural in paint and cut-out paper, and on this day Kitty and Tom and two other children were chosen to do special extra work on it.

Kitty was very excited. She loved painting – especially when you could be really messy.

That was why she wanted to paint the sky, with lovely big fluffy clouds floating along. But each time she tried Tom laughed at her. 'You can't reach,' he said. 'You're too small.' And he leaned over her head, and did the bit she wanted to do.

At break she found someone had put her

jacket on one of the higher pegs she could not reach, and she wouldn't ask Tom or anyone to get it down. So she went outside without it, and felt cold. Then the playground helper told her off for not wearing a coat.

'I couldn't reach it,' said Kitty, in a small voice.

'Oh, you're such a *dear little* thing,' said the lady, nicely.

Kitty sighed. It really was not fair.

Then it was the games lesson, when the girls had to play netball. They were learning to stop each other getting the ball. You had to dodge quickly, and jump very high. Kitty wasn't very good at that.

Today she was worse than ever. She did not get hold of the ball once. All the other girls had longer arms and legs, and it seemed easy for them. Afterwards one of the girls said something that hurt Kitty very much. 'No one will want you in their team, Kitty. You're too *tiny*!'

Kitty was very quiet when she got home. Her mum noticed. At last Kitty burst into tears. 'It's not fair that I'm little,' she sobbed.

Kitty told her mum everything. Mum nodded. 'It isn't easy. *I* was small when I was a little girl, and you ask Daniel what

9

they say to him in school!'

Surprised, Kitty went to find her big brother to ask him. He made a face. 'They sometimes call me Shorty,' he said. 'But it's always very friendly, so I don't mind!'

'Are you small too?' asked Kitty.

'Yes. But I'd rather be me than the boy in our class who's so tall and thin they call him Stringy!'

'You see,' said Mum, 'most people have got something about themselves they would like to change. When you know that, it makes you feel better about yourself.'

Kitty thought about that, and she made a plan. The next day, at playtime, she made herself feel brave enough to go up to Tom when he was standing on his own.

'Tom, can I ask you something?' she said.

'What, Shrimp?'

'If you had one wish, what would you change about yourself?'

The tall boy looked surprised. Then he went pink, and whispered, 'My hair. I *hate* my hair.' Kitty looked at it. It was orangey-brown. She thought it was rather nice.

'At my old school they called me Carrots,' he said, 'and it wasn't *fair*. But don't you tell anyone, will you – Shrimp?'

Kitty said she wouldn't.

Then she found Susie, the big strong girl who had said Kitty was no good at netball, and asked her the same question. Susie frowned, and answered quickly. 'My size,' she said, 'because I feel like an elephant. I'd like to be smaller. I'd like to be like *you*.'

'Like me?' squeaked Kitty, amazed.

Susie nodded.

Kitty looked round the playground, at all the children running around. Some tall, some small. Some fat, some thin. Some dark, some fair. Some shy, some bold. Some

who could sing, some who could swim.
Some dainty, some clumsy . . .

'We're *all* different,' she said to herself,
'and I suppose *that's* fair!'

It's not fair!

... that people can't take a joke

'Kitty! You're the naughtiest child in England!' said Mum.

'How do you know? You haven't met them all,' said Kitty.

'Oh, very clever,' said Mum, in her irritated voice.

'Thanks, Mum!' said Kitty.

Her mother opened her mouth – then closed it again. Kitty thought she looked like a fish, and said so. It made her laugh. Then

Mum got up from the table, and started to come towards her – so Kitty thought it was time to leave the room.

She ran into the hall, and up the stairs, bumping into Dad, who was walking down. He dropped his book with a crash, and it tumbled to the bottom of the stairs, bending its cover back.

'Oh, be careful, Kitty,' he shouted. 'Look where you're going!'

'*You* could see me coming,' retorted Kitty.

'That's not the point,' said Dad.

'Yes it is,' said Kitty, ''cos if *you* don't see, why should *I* look?'

Dad frowned. 'I'm not standing here arguing with you, Kitty,' he said, 'because I think you're a very cheeky little girl.'

And with that he stomped off down the stairs and closed the sitting-room door with a slam.

This time Kitty didn't laugh.

On the landing she met Daniel, her brother, coming out of his room wearing his new glasses. He didn't like his glasses, at all, even though he only really had to wear them for reading.

Kitty giggled.

'Hallo, *Wol*,' she said.

'What?' said Dan, puzzled.

14

'Wol,' she smiled. 'You know, in the Pooh Bear story – it's how poor old owl spelt his own name. WOL!' She giggled.

Daniel knew what she meant right away, and his face went red. 'I don't look like an owl,' he said, in his crossest voice. 'And even if I did you shouldn't say so. It's nasty.'

Then he rushed past her down the stairs, with angry clattering footsteps.

Kitty was still smiling, but the smile froze on her face. Slowly she walked into her own room, and looked into the mirror. She felt as if everybody in the house was against her.

The trouble with people (she thought) is that they never understand jokes. She wasn't trying to be nasty, or cheeky, or clever. She was only trying to be funny, and that was different.

'It's just not *fair*,' she said to her own frowning reflection. 'None of them can take a joke.'

Then she thought of the way Dad and Dan teased her, and expected her to smile with them . . . And it was then that Kitty had her Great Idea.

An hour later it was time for lunch. She heard Dad calling her name, and she went slowly downstairs, sitting at the table without a word.

Nobody in Kitty's house stayed cross for long, and so Dad smiled at her. 'What have you been doing upstairs, Kit?' he asked.

'Just reading,' she replied, in a polite, flat voice – not at all like her own, 'and tidying my room.'

'Gosh, are you feeling all right?' joked her mother, as she passed the plates.

'Oh yes, I'm fine, thank you,' said Kitty in the same voice.

Daniel looked at her strangely. He had taken his glasses off now, and seemed to have forgotten her joke. 'Do you want to play football after lunch?' he asked.

'No, thank you,' Kitty said quietly. 'I don't want to get dirty.'

All through the meal it was the same. Kitty was quiet and polite – and very, *very* dull. She never once smiled, or laughed, or giggled, or teased, or talked with her mouth full, or any of the things that made her *Kitty*. She said 'yes, please' and 'no, thank you' as if they were strangers and she had to be on her best behaviour.

By the time they had finished the meal, the other three were looking at her with astonishment.

'Are you sure you're not feeling poorly?' asked her mother, sounding really worried.

'You're not my normal little Kit,' said her dad.

'Kitty – you're being really *boring*,' grumbled Dan.

At that, Kitty got to her feet. 'Right!' she said, and folded her arms. 'Listen! When I'm being jokey and teasing you all, you don't like it. Then when I'm quiet and polite and serious you don't like that either. Do you think that's fair?'

'Er – no,' said Dad.

17

'Not really,' said Mum.

Daniel just shook his head.

Kitty was triumphant. 'There you are then,' she said. 'So you have to decide which sort of *me* you want to have around.

It's only fair.'

Dad smiled. 'Oh, I know what I think,' he said, and Mum smiled too, nodding before he had spoken. 'I'd rather have the Kitty who's the funniest girl in the world.'

'How do you know?' grinned Kitty.
''Cos you don't know all the rest!'

It's not fair!

. . . that he goes to bed late

It happened the same way every evening. Mum came into the sitting room and tapped Kitty on the shoulder. 'Time for bed, love,' she said.

Kitty scowled and pointed to where Dan was reading, or drawing or watching some television. 'Tell him, too,' she said.

Mum sighed. 'It's not Daniel's bed-time,' she said.

'That's not fair,' Kitty wailed. 'He always stays up later than me.'

'That's because he's older than you are,' said Mum. 'Honestly, Kitty, I shouldn't have to say that again.'

And then Kitty gave in, and went upstairs as slowly as possible, muttering dark things about her brother and how it wasn't fair that being older gave you treats – and so on.

But then came a night when the story was different. Two weeks earlier a new family

21

had moved in next door, and Kitty was pleased that amongst their three children was a boy who was exactly her age. He was called William. They liked the same games, and soon found out everything about each other.

So when Kitty's mother came to send her to bed Kitty looked up and said, 'It isn't fair.'

'I don't believe it!' said Mum. 'I've *told* you Dan is older and that's why . . .'

'Ah,' said Kitty. 'I'm not talking about him. I'm talking about William! He goes to bed only half an hour before Daniel does, and William is *exactly my age*.'

'Oh,' said Mum.

There was a short silence.

Kitty was triumphant. 'So I think I should be allowed to stay up as long as William.'

'All families have different rules, Kitty,' said Mum.

'I don't think that's fair,' said Kitty.

'Well, all children need different amounts of sleep,' said Mum, 'and that's got nothing to do with fairness!'

'Some people need to eat less food than others, too,' said Dad, from behind his newspaper.

All that week Kitty kept on. And on. Each night she complained. She asked Dad what he thought, and he agreed with Mum – of course. She asked Daniel – and he was on her side.

She even asked William's mother if she thought it was fair that she had to go to bed earlier than William. Mrs Jones looked embarrassed. 'That's up to your mummy, Kitty,' she said.

At last Kitty's mother could stand it no

longer. She had been busy and by Sunday night she was tired. So when Kitty started to say, 'Can't I stay up a little bit longer, as late as . . .' Mum interrupted.

'ALL RIGHT! We'll do an experiment. This week you can stay up till Dan's bed-time, which is later than William's. That way, he'll start telling *his* mum it's not fair, which will make a change – and *you* can see how much sleep you need.'

'Oh, Mum. THANKS,' Kitty gasped.

It was wonderful to stay up late that night – as if it was Christmas or New Year. Kitty felt very grown-up. And the next morning she didn't feel a bit tired. 'You see, I was right,' she said to Mum.

But on Tuesday Kitty had a bad day in school. She lost her pen, and somebody pushed her over in the playground, and she couldn't find her gym shoes, and – oh, lots of little things went wrong.

By the end of the afternoon her head was aching a bit, and she found herself thinking longingly of cuddling up with Mr Tubs in her little white bed. When the friendly clock on the mantelpiece showed her normal bed-time, Kitty nearly got up – then she remembered.

Dad and Mum were watching something boring on the television, and Daniel was doing his homework at the kitchen table.

Kitty stared at the screen, then at her book, but her head ached.

Still she wouldn't give in.

By the time it came to Thursday she felt tired. Very tired. 'Oh, Kitty, you've got dark circles under your eyes,' said her teacher.

'You keep yawning, Kitty,' said William – who looked as fresh as a daisy.

'Why don't *you* yawn?' she asked.

''Cos I'm not tired,' he said cheerfully.

'*Oh, I am!*' thought Kitty. But she didn't say it.

When Saturday morning came, Kitty slept and slept and slept.

She slept through her favourite cartoon programme on the television, which she was always allowed to watch.

She slept right through the cooked breakfast Mum always made on Saturday as a treat.

She slept, even though Dad called her loudly, and so he took Dan to the park for football without her.

By the time she came downstairs almost the whole of lovely Saturday morning had gone. The sun was shining in the garden, Dad and Daniel had gone – and Kitty felt she had missed out.

Mum was setting the table for lunch. She smiled at Kitty gently. 'It's not fair, you know,' she said.

'What's not fair?' Kitty asked.

'Well, what you've been doing is catching up on your sleep, because you simply haven't been giving yourself enough. And I don't think that's a *bit* fair, do you?'

'No,' said Kitty. 'It's not.'

It's not fair!

. . . that we can't stay

It was the summer holiday, and the most perfect one ever. Kitty's parents had rented a little cottage in the heart of the country. It wasn't big or grand: a sitting room, a kitchen, two little bedrooms and a bathroom under a thatched roof – that's all. But Kitty loved it.

She and Daniel had to share a room, which normally they hated – but that couldn't spoil their holiday. They hardly ever quarrelled – not *here*.

For two whole weeks she and Daniel ran wild, like little squirrels – climbing trees, playing hide-and-seek in the big garden, going for long walks in the woods with Mum and Dad.

'I've never had such a lovely time,' Kitty said.

But now it was the last day. Dad was sweeping the stone floor of the little kitchen,

and Mum was upstairs, packing their bags. It was over. And Kitty couldn't bear it.

Dad found her sitting by the sitting-room window, looking out across the fields, with a very sulky look on her face.

'Mum's calling you, Kit,' he said. 'You've to go and start packing your toys.'

Kitty said nothing.

'Come on – what's the matter?' asked Dad.

'Donwannagoback – noffair,' she mumbled, without turning round.

Dad laughed. 'What are you complaining about now?'

Kitty swung round to face him, and folded her arms. 'I said it's not fair we can't stay,' she said, crossly. 'I don't want to go back to our boring old house, in the boring old town, and go to boring old school. I want to stay here for ever and ever.'

'But you *can't*, Kit,' said Dad.

'I know – and it's not FAIR!' shouted Kitty, bursting into tears and running out of the room.

An hour later Dad carried the suitcases downstairs, and put them in the car. Daniel was helping. Mum was tidying the sitting room. But there was no sign of Kitty.

'Kitty!' Mum called, sounding worried.

'What's wrong?' asked Dad.

Mum rushed past him, and looked into the downstairs toilet. 'Oh, where *is* that girl?' she said.

They looked everywhere – under the beds, in the bathroom, in the wardrobe, behind the sofa, under the tables, even in the wicker basket on the landing. But there was no sign of Kitty.

Daniel called her name loudly.

'Oh . . . she wouldn't wander off and get

lost, would she?' Mum asked, in a very anxious voice.

'No way,' said Dad. 'She knows that would be wrong and silly, and I *know* she'd never do it. No – she's hiding, that's all. She doesn't want to go home.'

'Well, she's found a really good hiding place,' said Daniel, rather pleased at the thought that his sister was going to get into trouble.

'So how can we get her out of it?' murmured Dad. 'Hmm, maybe I've got a plan . . .'

At that moment Kitty was sitting in the one place they hadn't thought of looking: the little lean-to shed where old deck-chairs were kept. Or at least – Mum had just looked in quickly, peering through the dusty glass in the door. There was a spider's web over a hole in the glass. 'Ugh, Kitty would never go in there,' she thought.

But Kitty hid behind two stacked deck-chairs, feeling very pleased with herself. 'Now they won't be able to go,' she said to herself.

Just then she heard Dad calling. 'We're off now, Kit,' he shouted, 'so if you don't want to come with us, you can stay here.'

'Goodbye,' shouted Mum and Daniel.

'Ha, if they think I'd fall for that one . . .'

smiled Kitty. But then she heard the car
doors slam, then the engine start, and then
the sound of the car driving away. She
waited for a while, not believing what she
had heard.

It was quiet.

Very quiet.

Something rustled at the back of the shed,
and a spider ran across the floor.

Kitty decided she had been in there long enough.

She crept from her hiding place, and stood listening. Not a sound. The holiday cottage that had been full of family noise was now silent and empty, and Kitty didn't like it. But she knew she had to be brave.

'Right then, I'll go and read my book in the sitting room . . . then I'll go for a walk, then . . .' she said, in a small voice.

It was so *very* quiet.

Slowly she walked up to the back door and pushed it open. It was funny – she had never noticed it creak like that before. In the kitchen the tap went *drip, drip, drip*. It sounded awfully loud in the empty house.

'Oh, dear,' said Kitty. 'I don't think I like it here any more.'

But what was that? Was it a sound. . .?

Slowly she pushed open the door into the little sitting room, and there she saw . . . Mum, Dad and Daniel, sitting on the sofa, grinning at her.

'OH!' cried Kitty, and ran into Mum's arms.

'We knew you'd come out,' said Daniel.

'As if we'd go and leave you,' said Mum.

'We parked the car outside the gate, and crept back,' said Dad.

Kitty was so relieved she didn't say

another word about staying, and Mum and
Dad didn't tell her off for hiding.

But two weeks later it was her birthday.
And Mum and Dad's present was very big.

Kitty was thrilled to see her very own little
playhouse, with a painted thatched roof, and
painted roses round the door.

'There you are, Kit,' said Dad. 'Now
you've got your very own cottage, to have
holidays in all year round!'

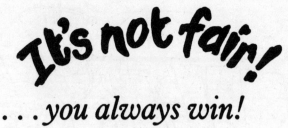

...*you always win!*

It was such fun having a new friend next door. Kitty and William got on really well – most of the time. Every Saturday morning one of them would squeeze through the hole in the fence, and soon they would have a good game going.

That is – until they quarrelled. And as they knew each other better they started to quarrel more and more. It wasn't that they liked each other less. It was just that they were too alike. And both of them wanted to win. All the time.

Kitty would often come back from William's house sulking.

'Had one of your tiffs, dear?' Mum would say.

'They're just like an old married couple,' teased Dad – which made Kitty crosser than ever.

But soon she or William would feel bored.

So one of them would squeeze through the hole in the fence – and soon they would be playing again.

On this particular Saturday it was pouring with rain. Kitty pulled on her anorak, picked up a carrier-bag, stuffed it full of games, told her mum where she was going, and ran next door.

'What shall we play?' asked William.

'Snakes and ladders,' said Kitty.

But the red counter Kitty chose always seemed to land on snakes' heads, whilst

William's blue counter climbed up ladder after ladder.

At last – 'I've won!' – he cried.

Kitty said nothing – even when he won the second game as well.

Then they tried Ludo. This time Kitty chose blue for luck, and William swapped to green. But however hard she shook the dice, Kitty kept throwing ones and twos, whilst William threw sixes. The green counters raced around the board, and landed home, whilst the blue counters just couldn't get going.

At last – 'I've won!' – he cried.

Kitty said nothing, but her mouth turned down.

'What about snap?' asked William with a grin.

'Oh, all right,' sighed Kitty.

It was hopeless. William spotted the pairs so quickly, and yelled, 'SNAP!' so loudly – and soon he was sweeping up the pile. Kitty threw down her last card. Her face went red.

'It's not fair!' she shouted. 'You *always* win!'

'That's because I'm clever,' said William with a grin, flicking the pack of cards.

Kitty was so disappointed she wanted to cry.

Just then William's big sister Sally walked

past. She was thirteen, and *very* grown-up, and Kitty thought she was wonderful. Sally liked Kitty too – and she heard what William said.

'That's rubbish, Will,' she said. 'It's got nothing to do with being clever. You're just lucky.'

'No, it's *skill*,' boasted William.

'Doesn't take any skill to throw a dice,' snorted Sally.

'Whatever it is, it's *not fair*,' wailed Kitty.

'Crybaby,' said William.

At that, Sally took hold of Kitty's hand, and led her upstairs without another word. Her room was marvellous; full of beads and books and ornaments, with posters of pop singers and Sally's own bright paintings on the walls.

'Now,' said Sally, taking out a little chess set. 'William's just learning this. Can you play?'

'Dad started to show me, but . . .'

'Right. Now, you remember how each piece moves. . .?'

Kitty remembered, and soon she was absorbed in the game. Sally told her how to work out moves well in advance, and how to guess what the other person would do, and

when to move the King and the Queen. It was such fun – like fitting together the pieces in a jigsaw puzzle. Kitty loved it.

After nearly an hour had passed, Sally said, 'Now you go downstairs and challenge William.'

Kitty did just that.

They played in silence, concentrating really hard. At last William looked up with a frown. 'You're *winning*,' he said – as if he didn't believe it.

'Checkmate!' said Kitty.

'Not fair . . .' William started to moan.

'Too right!' said Kitty. 'It's jolly unfair that *some* of us have all the skill!'

It's not fair!

... that things aren't fair

It was a cold morning in November, and Kitty and her mum were walking along a busy road. They were going to see Gran, who lived in a special home for old people. Kitty liked visiting Gran. She always had a roll of sweets in her pocket.

Suddenly Kitty heard the sound of music. On the corner of the street stood an old man, playing a mouth organ. His clothes were worn. In front of him, on the pavement, was a battered hat, in which some people had put money.

He didn't play the mouth organ very well, and that made Kitty feel even more sorry for him.

'Mum, can we put some money in his hat?' she whispered.

'Of course,' said Mum, and pulled a silver coin from her pocket. Kitty felt embarrassed as she threw it down, and ran off quickly.

'Why is he poor, Mum?' Kitty asked.

'I don't know, love.'

Kitty said nothing.

As they waited to cross the road she noticed a huge poster on the wall opposite. It showed some children who were very, very thin, and was asking people to send money to help those children.

'Do they live in Africa, Mum?' Kitty asked.

Mum nodded. 'Well, *why* haven't they got enough food?' asked Kitty. '*We* have, so why haven't they?'

Mum sighed. 'Oh, I don't really know, Kitty. Sometimes it's because of the weather . . . it's all so complicated.'

Kitty said nothing.

Gran was in a good mood. She sat knitting, and her eyes sparkled when she saw them. 'How's my untidy little girl?' she said, reaching out to ruffle Kitty's hair.

'What are you knitting, Nana?' Kitty asked.

Gran held up a long shapeless-looking jumper. 'It's for your dad,' she said. 'It's his Christmas present.' Kitty imagined Dad wearing it, and giggled.

Soon she was quietly munching sweets, as Mum and Gran talked. But then she noticed that Gran didn't look so cheerful any more.

She was saying that she hadn't been well, and added, 'Don't worry, it's just old age, that's all.'

'You're not old, Gran – not *really* old,' Kitty said.

'Oh yes, I am,' sighed Gran.

Kitty wanted to go home, but felt guilty for thinking it. Later, when they did leave, she didn't want to look at all the other old ladies, waiting for their visitors. It made her feel sad.

All the way home she said nothing.

When they were sitting at the kitchen table Mum said, 'Come on now, Kit, what's the matter?'

'Why do people have to grow old? I don't want *you* to get old,' Kitty said.

'But I have to,' smiled Mum. 'We all have to.'

'Why can't we just all stay as we are?'

'Because we can't. It's not possible.'

Suddenly Kitty felt angry. She banged the table with her fist, so that all the cups and plates rattled.

'IT'S NOT FAIR!' she shouted.

'What isn't?' asked Mum.

'EVERYTHING. I feel so sorry for people like that poor man in the street, and then I think that we've got so much more than all those people in Africa and India, and I don't know why we haven't all got the same. And then Gran isn't very well, and I know she hates being old and not being able to do things . . . It's just not . . .'

Kitty felt like crying.

'Come on my knee,' said Mum. They had a big cuddle, then she whispered, 'Things do seem very unfair, don't they, love?'

Kitty nodded. 'But *why*, Mum?'

'I can't tell you. There isn't a grown-up in the world who could tell you the answer,' said Mum.

'I thought grown-ups knew everything,' sighed Kitty.

Mum shook her head. 'No, love. Oh, I *could* tell you that if we weren't so selfish we could give more to poor people – whether they live here or the other side of the world.

But there's more to it than that. And in any case, that wouldn't stop people being ill or old, would it?'

Kitty shook her head.

'I wish that *everything* was fair,' she said.

'So do I,' said Mum. 'But it can't be.'

'It still makes me cross,' said Kitty.

'And it probably always will,' said Mum.

It's not fair!

... she's got more presents

Christmas was the best day of the whole year, of course, and this time it seemed better than ever. Kitty's stocking had been crammed with funny little toys and jokes.

And after breakfast, when they opened their main presents, Kitty was so pleased. Mum and Dad had bought her what she most wanted: a huge art set, with lots of different paints, paper of all sizes, felt-tips, crayons, pencils and rubbers – all packed into a lovely carrying case.

She had plenty of books too, because she loved reading, and a lovely long scarf from Gran, in rainbow colours. Dan gave her three more soldiers and horses for her castle. She was very happy.

Kitty and Daniel were sorry about one thing, though.

This year Mum and Dad had arranged to go to have Christmas dinner with Aunty

Susan and Uncle Joe. *That* wasn't so bad, although they said they would rather have their own turkey.

But going to that house meant something that made them both moan.

'*Melissa*,' said Daniel, making a rude face.

'Yuk,' said Kitty.

They had to leave all the lovely clutter of wrapping paper and ribbons and glittery pom-poms, and go out. 'Aunty Susan's house is so *tidy*,' groaned Kitty in the car.

'Just like Melissa. Maybe she vacuum-cleans Melissa when she does the carpets,' grinned Dan.

Kitty giggled.

'That's enough,' said Dad.

There was a delicious smell of food when Aunty Susan opened the door. They all said Happy Christmas and hugged each other, although Daniel and Kitty ducked out of hugging their cousin.

'Why don't all the children play upstairs till dinner's ready?' said Uncle Joe.

But Dan asked if he could practise on his new skateboard on the garden path, and so Kitty was left with Melissa.

'Don't you like to wear your best dress on Christmas Day,' asked Melissa, 'instead of old jeans?'

'They aren't *old*, they're my new cords,' said Kitty indignantly. 'And this is a new jumper.'

'It wasn't a good start.

'Oh, well, I suppose you'd like to see all my presents,' said Melissa, throwing open her bedroom door.

Kitty gasped.

There was a toy cooker with plastic pots and pans, and a multi-way pram for Melissa's dolls, and a little pink wardrobe crammed with dolls' clothes on hangers, and a hairstyling set with pink plastic rollers, brushes and combs, and a funny dummy-head to work on.

'Who gave you all those?' asked Kitty.

'Mummy and Daddy. And I've got lots of

ordinary things like paints and books from
aunties and uncles.'

'Gosh,' said Kitty.

'What did you get?' asked Melissa.

Kitty told her.

'Is that *all*?' asked her cousin.

Suddenly Kitty felt like a balloon that has

gone pop. The turkey tasted delicious, and the crackers were fun, and Aunty Susan and Uncle Joe gave her a big notice-board in the shape of an elephant for her bedroom.

'So you can pin up your lists,' said Aunty Susan, picking up the paper right away and folding it neatly.

'Then you won't forget things,' smiled Uncle Joe.

Everybody laughed. Except Kitty.

At last it was time to go home. Kitty was glad to get back to their own comfortable, messy house. But Mum and Dad could tell that something was bothering her.

She sat by the Christmas tree, looking up at the coloured lights. And one thought was going through her mind – something so bad she wouldn't have told it to anyone. *'It's not fair she's got more presents than me.'* That was what Kitty thought.

Just then Dan came up. 'What did you think of Melissa's stuff then?' he asked.

'She had lots of nice presents,' said Kitty, in a small voice.

Daniel threw back his head and laughed. 'What? All those nimsy-mimsy things in pink plastic for dolly-wollies? Not your sort of thing, Kit. You've got more taste.'

And Kitty realised he was right. There wasn't a *single* thing in Melissa's room that she would have wanted. Not one.

She stared up at the tree again. It had a warm, Christmassy smell. Already, showers of little pine needles fell down when you touched it.

Aunty Susan had an artificial tree because she said real ones made too much mess. And they didn't have paper chains in each room, or a Christmas Candle in the window, dropping wax all over the place, but giving a warm welcoming glow.

Kitty grinned slowly.

'Our tree is *much* better than Melissa's tree,' she said.

And *Melissa* might have said, 'Not fair!'

It's not fair!

. . . I have to do all the work

'It's your turn.'

'No, it isn't. I did it yesterday.'

'But you said you'd make up for that time last week when you went out.'

'Nonsense.'

It wasn't Kitty and Daniel who were squabbling. It was Mum and Dad. And Kitty and Daniel couldn't bear it.

They were arguing over who did the washing-up. Usually they took turns, but lately things had got mixed up – and now they were very cross with each other.

'Tired! Huh! It's just not fair that I have to do all the work,' said Mum.

'What do you think I do all day?' said Dad.

And so they went on.

And on.

Kitty and Daniel were listening in the hall. 'I wish they'd shut up,' said Dan.

'So do I,' said Kitty. 'Why do parents have to argue?'

Daniel shrugged. 'Dunno . . . I suppose it's because they're just the same as us, underneath.'

Then Mum swept past them, slamming the kitchen door behind her. 'I'm going out to my class, kids,' she said. 'Bye.'

A few minutes later Dad stomped from the kitchen. 'You can start getting yourself to bed now, Kitty, and it's time you did your homework, Dan,' he said grumpily. 'I'm going out into the garage to mend the car radio.'

'All right, Dad,' they said together.

Five minutes later Kitty crept out of her bedroom. She knew what she had to do.

First she lifted up the laundry basket and half-carried, half-dragged it downstairs. One or two socks fell out along the way, but Kitty didn't notice.

In the kitchen she stuffed as many clothes as she could into the washing machine, and grabbed the powder. 'How much do you put in?' she wondered, then shrugged and poured a pile into the little compartment.

'One less job for Mum to do,' she said.

Then she took a chair and climbed up by the sink. A good, long squeeze of washing-up liquid . . . and a mountain of bubbles filled the sink. With a clatter Kitty swept all the dirty dishes into it.

Water and soap bubbles splashed on to the floor, but Kitty didn't mind. Her clothes were soaked, but it didn't matter. She piled all the washing-up anyhow on the draining-board, breaking just one cup. Only one. Then it was done. 'One less job for Dad to do,' she said.

What next? She looked around. The washing machine was making odd noises, and more bubbles were creeping from under its door. Never mind.

She decided to set the table ready for

59

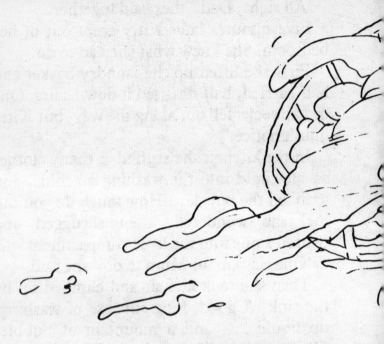

breakfast. But since all the usual dishes were on the draining-board in a *very* unsafe pile, she went to the sideboard and got out the best china and cutlery.

That was another job done. Now what? Mum was always saying the fridge needed a clear-out. So Kitty decided to do that – to be really helpful.

First you had to take everything out – but there was nowhere to put it really, except the table. And that was already laid for breakfast. Oh, never mind . . .

So Kitty put the milk bottles, orange

juice, butter, eggs, and everything else on the table amongst the best china. And only one egg got broken. Just one.

She wiped down the shelves, and then left the fridge and freezer doors open wide. She had seen Mum do that. That was another job they wouldn't have to do.

After that Kitty went into the sitting room and plumped up all the cushions, pummelling them furiously so that clouds of dust rose into the air.

She ran the carpet-sweeper over the hall carpet, but forgot to put it away.

She grabbed the feather duster and attacked all the pictures, knocking most of them sideways as she did so.

And when Mum came through the front door, not long afterwards, Kitty was sitting on the floor surrounded by a pile of shoes, waving a brush, with polish all over her face and hands – and a lot of it on the floor too.

Dad must have heard Mum, because just then he came in through the back door. 'I just wanted to say I'm sor . . .' he began, then stopped. He looked around the kitchen in horror.

'What on earth has been going on?' he said.

Kitty beamed. 'Well,' she said, 'I hate it when you argue. And since you both think it's not fair that you have to do so much work, I thought I'd help you. *I've* done all the work!'

Dad went across and put his arms around Mum, who looked as though she might faint. They stared at each other for a long time. And then they began to laugh. And laugh.

'Are you pleased?' asked Kitty.

'Y-y-yes, darling,' spluttered Mum.

'And so you promise you'll never argue again?' said Kitty wagging her finger at them.

'If you'll never do the work again. Fair enough!' said Dad.

To Adam Kington

But you promised!

. . . I could have a pet

'But you *promised* I could have a pet,' wailed Kitty.

'No I didn't,' said Mum firmly. 'Not a proper promise. I just said . . .'

'You said I could have a dog for Christmas – you DID!'

Kitty was cross and disappointed. Mum and Dad had said she could have a pet for Christmas, and she and Daniel had decided a dog would be most fun. But now Mum had a job, and so she said it would be too much trouble. 'I'll have so much to do, Kitty,' she sighed. 'You must understand.'

But Kitty only understood one thing. 'You *said* we'd get a dog, and Dad said he'd like one too, didn't you Dad?'

'Well, yes, I did,' said Dad.

'I want us to have a pet. All the boys in

school have animals. And I'd help Kitty look after it,' said Daniel.

'But puppies need training, and dogs have to be taken for walks, and dog food has to be bought – and who'd do all that?' asked Mum. 'I wanted this job so much, and it means I'll have less time to do all the things I have to do.'

'What about a little kitten?' asked Kitty, in a small voice.

'I don't want extra chores,' said Mum firmly. 'I'm sorry.' She sounded cross, but a bit guilty too.

Kitty looked furious.

Dan looked disappointed.

'Oh dear,' said Dad.

Kitty turned and ran from the room, not minding that she made all the decorations on the tree shiver as she passed. Up in her room she picked up Mr Tubs and hugged him. 'Grown-ups *never* keep their promises,' she whispered. 'So it looks as if we won't get our puppy, Mr T.'

She thought for a moment. 'Never mind, he might have tried to play with you and torn you by accident . . .'

Mr Tubs had lovely soft fur and a wonderful smell, and he always made Kitty feel better. If she was cross or sad or worried, all she had to do was pick up her favourite bear and squeeze him tightly, and soon she would think of a good game to play, and forget her troubles.

'You always give me ideas, Mr Tubs,' said Kitty slowly. It was happening now . . . the soft fur . . . the friendly brown eyes . . . Yes! Kitty had a brilliant plan.

She went to empty her money-box. There

wasn't much inside, because she had done most of her Christmas shopping. But there were still some coins left, and Kitty knew she could borrow some from Dad. And there were three more days until Christmas day . . .

On Christmas morning Daniel and Kitty opened their stockings early. It seemed a long wait until after breakfast, when they could have the presents under the tree. Lovely mysterious parcels in strange shapes . . . Kitty was so excited, she even forgot to be disappointed that there was nothing which yapped or miaowed.

At last it was present time. After they had opened a few gifts from aunts and uncles, Dan turned to Kitty with a grin and said, 'Here you are, Kit – open mine.'

It was small and squashy. Kitty pulled off all the paper in a rush – and there was a little, cuddly brown felt dog, with floppy ears.

'It's a pet for you, Kit,' said Dan.

Kitty couldn't believe it. She hugged her brother, then handed him her parcel. It was medium-sized and squashy. Daniel pulled off all the paper in a rush – and there was a cuddly black and white furry dog, with pointed ears and a pink felt tongue.

'It's a mascot for you, Dan – because you wanted a pet, too,' said Kitty.

'Help! We could open a pet shop,' smiled Dad. Then Mum handed him a parcel. It was

quite large, and squashy. Dad pulled off all the paper in a rush – and there was a big, grey, cuddly dog with hair all over its black glass eyes, and big paws.

'It's my little joke present, dear,' Mum said, 'because I decided you wanted a pet as much as the children did!'

Dad, Daniel and Kitty looked at each other, and at the three toy dogs – and then they laughed and laughed.

'Now,' said Mum. 'Open this, Kitty.' She handed Kitty a small white envelope.

On a piece of paper inside was this rhyme:

An empty bed, for friends to stay,

Is where you'll find a friend today

'That's easy,' said Kitty, 'It's the spare room. But what. . . ?'

Dad was smiling. 'Go and see,' he said.

Kitty ran upstairs, and they all followed her. She pushed open the spare-room door – and gasped. There, on the bed, was a large square cage, with an enormous ribbon wrapped round it, and a large label saying, 'Happy Christmas, Kitty, love from Mum and Dad.'

Inside was the tiniest, sweetest, prettiest baby hamster. She was honey-coloured, with bright eyes and neat little whiskers. When she heard them, she ran into her little house and peeped out nervously.

'Oh . . . oh . . . OH!' gasped Kitty. She was so pleased, she couldn't speak.

'What are you going to call her, Kit?' asked Daniel.

'Oh – I don't know. What about Sandy – 'cos she's that sort of colour?' Kitty said.

'That's a lovely name,' said Mum.

'But . . . but . . . why did you change your mind, Mum?' asked Kitty, running to hug her.

'I didn't change my mind, I just kept a promise,' said Mum.

'Anyway, hamsters are easy to look after,' said Dad. 'But you've got to promise to do it *properly*.'

73

Kitty opened the cage door, stretched out a hand, and stroked Sandy very gently on the nose with her finger. Who wouldn't keep a promise like that?

But you promised!

. . . *You wouldn't be cross*

It was one of those bad days. Kitty never knew how they began. Dad said it was because of getting out of bed the wrong side, but Kitty knew that was impossible. Her bed was up against the wall.

Whatever the reason, everything was going wrong. Kitty didn't want to do anything, and she lost things, and she thought that nothing seemed fair . . . but no matter how bad-tempered she got, Mum and Dad took no notice.

'What's wrong with Mum and Dad?' she asked her brother.

'They're in a good mood,' said Dan, 'but you wouldn't understand that, Kitty.'

'Why not?'

'Because you don't know what a good mood is!' He laughed, stuck out his tongue at her,

75

and ran away.

Kitty was very, very cross. She chased her brother out of the kitchen, and along the hall. But he was too quick for her, and darted out through the front door.

'Stupid brothers!' said Kitty, and went into the living room, slamming the door behind her. And that was when it started . . .

Kitty slammed the door so hard it made the room shake, and a big old vase on the table by the door trembled, and fell over. It cracked into three big pieces – but worse than that, it

fell against Sandy's cage, which was right at the edge of the table.

Crash! – the cage fell to the ground. The little door flew open and a terrified hamster scuttled out, moving faster than Kitty had ever seen her move before. 'Stop, Sandy!' Kitty yelled, and dived down to try to catch her. Sandy slipped through her hands like a bar of wet soap – but Kitty knocked over the round table with all its little photographs in frames.

'Sandy!' Kitty cried, crawling on her hands and knees and seeing her pet disappear behind the sofa. In a panic she pulled all the cushions off, and piled them at the other end so Sandy could not get out. Then, puffing and blowing, she pulled the sofa away from the wall – knocking over the standard lamp. The standard lamp in turn knocked over a vase of flowers, and all the water poured on to Mum's new rug . . .

The room was a mess, but Kitty didn't notice. All she could think was that if Sandy went down a hole in the skirting board she would be lost forever.

But it was all right. She made a last grab, and held her hamster tightly in her hands. In a moment Sandy was back safely in her cage – and it was then Kitty looked around. And she heard Mum and Dad come in through the

kitchen door from the garden.

She was smiling sweetly when she went through the kitchen door. 'What's wrong?' asked Dad.

'You've had a change of mood,' said Mum.

'Mum and Dad, you know I think you're the best parents in the world?'

'Ye-es,' they said together, smiling.

'Well, if I tell you something, promise you won't be cross?'

'Oh, it's too nice a day to be bad-tempered,' laughed Dad, 'so what is it?'

'Sandy escaped, and I made a bit of a mess in the living room trying to catch her,' said Kitty.

'Oh, not to worry. What's a little mess?' said Mum, cheerfully.

But when they opened the living-room door and saw the chaos, Mum's face fell.

'Good heavens, Kitty, do you call this a LITTLE mess?' roared Dad, going very red.

'But you promised not to be cross,' said Kitty.

'We hadn't *seen* it then!' said Mum, staring around with horror. 'Oh, Kitty, when I get my hands on you . . .'

Kitty went backwards down the hall. 'But you said . . .'

'Never mind that,' said Dad. 'I'll tell you what. We won't be cross if you promise to do whatever we say.'

'Oh, yes,' said Kitty.

'Right, then,' he said, 'TIDY THE ROOM.'

'On my *own*?'

They nodded, looking stern.

Kitty groaned. 'But . . .'

' . . . You *promised*!' they both said.

But you promised!

. . . It wouldn't hurt

Kitty was hiding. She could hear Mum calling her, and Dad telling Dan to look in the toy cupboard. But she stuffed her fingers in her ears and closed her eyes, and wished, wished, *wished* that they would all go away.

'KITTY!' called Mum.

'NO – I won't, I won't,' whispered Kitty to herself.

The trouble was this. Kitty had to go to the doctor to have an injection, and she didn't want to go. So while the family was having breakfast she crept under the pretty cloth that covered a little round table on the landing – right to the ground. It was such an obvious place to hide that Mum, Dad and Dan rushed past it, looking for her.

At last she heard Mum say that she had to go to work, and Dan say he had to go to school.

Dad had taken time off work to go with Kitty – and so now she held her breath, and closed her eyes, waiting for him to find her.

He stood by the table. She could see his feet. 'Now, where can my naughty girl be . . .?' he said to himself. There was a pause.

Then Kitty opened her eyes – to see Dad's face peering under the cloth at her. 'Come on out, Kit!' he grinned.

Five minutes later she was sitting at the kitchen table, while Dad made her some toast. 'Oh, Dad, I don't want to go to the doctor's,' she wailed.

'Why not?' he asked.

'Because it's an injection, and I hate them. I hate needles going into me.'

'But they do it so's you won't get really ill later,' said Dad, 'It's a good thing.'

'I don't care, I hate them,' scowled Kitty. 'And it will hurt. So I'm *not* going!'

'Yes, you are,' said Dad, pulling her to her feet, 'because it's important and, anyway, it won't hurt – I promise you.'

'Are you sure?' asked Kitty.

Dad nodded.

It seemed such a long time in the waiting room. Kitty tried to look at an Annual, but the pages were torn. And a baby was screaming on its mother's knees, and she couldn't concentrate – and she felt SO nervous.

At last they were called. Dad held her hand and they walked into the surgery. Dr Scott smiled at them, but Kitty didn't smile back. She knew the doctor was a jolly, kind lady who always gave children a sweet from the jar on her desk. She knew that it was important to have injections. But still she didn't smile.

'Oh, what a gloomy face,' smiled Dr Scott.

'I told her it won't hurt,' said Dad.

'Of course it won't,' said Dr Scott. 'Now just roll up your sleeve, Kitty. We'll just wipe the place to make it clean, like *that*, and you'll

feel a little tiny prick, like *that* . . .'

'OWW!' yelled Kitty.

She didn't cry – of course not. But she rubbed her arm, glared at Dr Scott and at Dad, and her mouth turned down at the corners. Dr Scott gave her a sweet and patted her on the head, saying she was a good girl – but Kitty was not happy.

When they got home, Dad made them a cup of tea. 'We'd better be quick, love. You've already missed half the morning's school. And I've got to get to work,' he said.

Kitty looked at him without smiling. 'It's

not fair, Dad,' she said. 'You said it wouldn't
hurt, and it *did* hurt.'

'Oh, Kit, it didn't hurt very much,' he said.

'How do you know? You weren't inside my
arm!' she replied. 'Anyway, you promised me
it wouldn't hurt.'

Dad sat down at the table and sipped his tea,
looking at her kindly. Then he put the mug
down and shook his head. 'Now, Kit,' he said.
'You *know* parents aren't in charge of
everything! There's a lot of things we can't
control – like whether people are nice to you at
school, or whether it will rain on sports day, or
whether you'll hurt a little bit at the doctor or
the dentist. You know that, don't you?'

'Well you shouldn't have promised,' said Kitty sternly.

Dad hugged her so hard she had to smile. 'Oh, Kit-Kat,' he said. 'One thing you'll have to learn – when grown-ups say "I promise" they usually mean "I hope"!'

But you promised!

. . . I could stay the night

There was a craze at Kitty's school for staying the night with friends, but Kitty had never done it. Nobody had asked her. Daniel said it was because all the mums had heard how naughty she was. Kitty didn't think that was funny.

'*You* have to arrange it, Mum,' she said. 'You ring up Jane's mother, or Kate's, and then they ask me to stay the night.'

'All right, dear,' her Mum said, in that voice which sounds as if it is thinking of something else. 'We'll see.'

'Oh *why* do grown-ups always say that?' Kitty asked.

'All right, I promise you I'll arrange something – will that do?'

'Huh,' was all Kitty said.

Three days later it was Friday. The end of

the week always made Kitty feel cheerful. She
was collected from school by William's
mother, and she and William were planning to
have a great game involving their two gardens
– when Kitty stopped dead in the street.

'Oh, no!' she said, staring at the car outside
her house. It was Aunty Susan's car – and that
meant one thing. Melissa.

'Quick – run into our garden, and then they
won't see you,' hissed William. He knew all
about Kitty's cousin. But it was too late.

Kitty's Mum was beckoning from the window. So Kitty had to say goodbye to William and walk up her own path.

'Isn't this a lovely surprise?' said Kitty's Mum, gaily. 'Aunty Susan and Melissa have popped in for tea.'

'Uh,' said Kitty, chewing her fingers.

'Gosh, aren't your nails dirty?' said Melissa.

'Uh,' said Kitty.

'Kitty, can't you talk properly?' said her Mum.

'Nuh,' said Kitty.

'*Kitty*!' said Mum.

Aunty Susan took no notice. She was used to Kitty, and just ruffled her hair, making it messier than ever. (Melissa's hair was in two tight plaits, with pink and white checked ribbons.) 'Anyway, Kitty, before you came home, we made a lovely plan. You're coming back with us to stay the night!'

Kitty gulped. 'Tonight?'

Mum and Aunty Susan nodded.

'There you are, Kit,' Mum said. 'I've been promising you could stay the night with someone, and thanks to Aunty Susan we've got it organised.'

Kitty knew that when Mum spoke in that bright, loud voice there was no point in arguing.

It only took a few minutes for Mum to run upstairs and pack Kitty's bag – while Kitty sat nibbling a biscuit and feeling gloomy. Melissa beamed at her. 'Aren't you going to comb your hair before we go?' she asked.

Melissa's house was like Melissa – everything in place, everything very *nice*, but nothing inviting you to play and have a really good time. *Just* like Melissa.

All Kitty's cousin wanted to do was watch television – which Kitty thought boring. Or play with dolls – which Kitty thought even

more boring. She thought longingly of William's wild garden next door, and the amazing adventurous games they made up.

'It's time for bed,' said Aunty Susan. Kitty looked at the clock. She couldn't believe it.

'But it's Friday,' she said.

'Never mind, dear, girls still need their beauty sleep,' said Aunty Susan, kindly.

'*Yuk*,' thought Kitty.

She couldn't say 'No' because she was a guest – and she knew that guests don't argue. So Kitty trailed upstairs after Melissa, and was forced to have a bath. 'I like lots of scented bubbles in my baths,' said Melissa.

So Kitty allowed herself to be scrubbed, and her hair to be washed, and her nails cut – just like Melissa. They were wrapped in clean white towels. Then the hairdryer roared at them both, and Aunty Susan got busy with the brush – until at last Kitty hardly recognized herself in the mirror.

'Where's your nightie, Kitty?'

Kitty pulled on Dan's old pyjamas, with the picture of Superman on the front, and Melissa looked at her scornfully. *She* was wearing a long white nightdress with lacy frills. Kitty thought she looked like a ghost, and wanted to giggle. Then – 'Oh, NO!' cried Kitty.

'What?', said Melissa and her Mum together.

'Mum forgot to put Mr Tubs in my bag. I can't sleep without him.'

'Never mind, dear, here's one of Melissa's lovely dolls for you to cuddle,' said Aunty Susan, tucking Kitty into bed.

She put a story tape on for them to listen to – but Kitty thought it was babyish. She preferred reading, or talking. She lay uncomfortably next to the blonde doll with hard arms and legs, staring blue eyes, and fancy clothes which tickled. 'I *hate* you, doll,' she whispered, giving it a shove under the bedclothes.

Kitty missed home. She thought of her own messy bedroom, in her own cosy house, and of Mr Tubs, and of the fun of Saturday mornings when she and Dan and the children next door all played together . . .

'Mum?' she said inside her head. 'Can you hear me? I never want to stay the night away – not ever again!'

But you promised!

. . . *You wouldn't tell*

Dad was going to be in charge. It happened a lot nowadays, because Kitty's Mum's new job meant that sometimes she had to work on Saturdays. Once they got used to it, Kitty and Daniel didn't mind. They always had fun with Dad.

This Saturday morning, Mum was in a bossy mood. 'There's plenty of salad in the fridge for lunch,' she said, 'and I want you to eat it up.'

The children groaned.

'Rabbit food,' said Daniel.

'I don't want to eat silly, slimy salad,' said Kitty.

'Can't we have something else?' they moaned.

But Mum had become very keen on really healthy eating and insisted, 'It's *good* for you

94

all – but if you want something hot to go with it, Dad can cook you some rice. But remember, NO biscuits for elevenses. They're bad for your teeth.'

They groaned even more loudly. But Mum took no notice, just grabbed her coat, and left.

Dad shrugged. 'Better do as we're told, kids.'

Kitty stuck out her teeth, held two fingers above her head like ears and hopped around. 'I'll turn into a bunny if I eat any more lettuce, Dad!' she said.

He laughed, and sent them out into the garden to play while he did the washing up.

The morning passed quickly. Daniel and Kitty played hide-and-seek with William and Sally, the children next door, until heavy clouds made the sky dark. Kitty shivered.

'It's going to rain,' said Sally. 'Come in for a snack.'

Her mother gave them a plate of chocolate biscuits to share, and glasses of lemonade. Daniel winked at Kitty.

As lunch-time came near they decided they should go home. It had stopped raining, but the air was damp and cold. 'Lovely weather for salad,' Kitty groaned.

They were surprised to see a strange man sitting at the kitchen table with Dad. They each had a glass of beer. Dad looked very pleased. He told the children this was a very old friend he hadn't seen for years. The man, whose name was Bill, was big and jolly. He looked at his watch, 'Well, if your lady-wife isn't coming home, why don't we all go down the road and get fish and chips?'

The children jumped up and down,

screaming with delight, and clapping their hands.

Dad looked at them, then at the fridge door, then at his watch. 'We-ell . . .'

'Oh, come on!' said Bill.

'You'd better promise not to tell your Mum,' said Dad.

'We won't!' yelled Kitty.

Twenty minutes later they were all walking down the road, munching delicious fish and chips with their fingers. When they got back to the house Bill took cans of fizzy drink from his pockets, which made a perfect end to the meal. The children were sorry when he had to go.

'Oh, dear,' said Dad, looking at the mess of greasy newspaper and empty cans on the kitchen table. 'We'd better clear up. Mum will be back in half an hour.'

When Mum's key turned in the lock, Dad and Daniel were watching a film on television, and Kitty was wheeling Mr Tubs up and down the hall on her old baby tricycle.

Mum kissed her. 'Hello, love, have you had a lovely day?'

Kitty nodded. She started to feel a bit guilty.

'And it wasn't *so* bad to have salad for lunch, was it?' asked Mum.

Kitty looked at her and went red. It was no good. She couldn't tell fibs – that would be terrible. So she told Mum what had happened.

'Aha – he did, did he?' said Mum, folding her arms, a little smile curling at the corner of her mouth. She marched into the sitting room.

'Well, was it good, having a salad of fish and chips?' she asked, standing in between Dad and the TV.

Dad looked really guilty. He glanced sideways at Kitty, and she could almost hear him thinking, *'But you promised you wouldn't tell.'*

'Don't be cross with Dad,' she said.

At that, a big grin broke across Mum's face. 'Look at you all!' she said. 'Like frightened rabbits! You obviously *have* been eating too many greens. Well, if you must know I went to the market to get a special treat for tonight's supper, and I met Bill – which was a lovely surprise. And he told me about your lunch.'

'And you don't mind?' asked Dad.

'Course not. I'm not a witch, you know! Didn't I say I'm making something you like for supper?'

'What is it, Mum?' asked Kitty.

'Fish and chips!' said Mum.

'Oh, no!' they all groaned. And then they started to laugh.

But you promised!

. . . You'd choose me

There was a new girl in Kitty's class. She was called Rosie, and she was very nice. On her first day she was put next to Kitty, who had to show her where everything was – they quickly became friends.

Rosie had short black curly hair, and laughed a lot. Very soon the teacher discovered that she was clever in lessons, as well as good at games.

'Oh, Rosie, you're so lucky,' Kitty sighed one day, 'because you're good at everything!'

'It's not *luck*,' Rosie said with a grin. 'It's hard work!'

Rosie and Kitty did everything together. They shared their biscuits at break, swapped books they liked, and chose each other as partners in gym and dancing.

'Will you always choose me, Rosie?' Kitty

asked – rather proud because her friend was
better than all the rest.

'Course I will, silly.'

'Promise?'

'Cross my heart.'

Kitty was happy. She had always wanted a
really *best* friend. It didn't matter that Rosie
was a faster runner, or could dive like a fish.

They were friends. And that was more important than anything.

Or so Kitty thought – until the week before Sports Day.

Kitty didn't like Sports Day because, she said to Mum, 'It's no fun running a race and seeing all the others in front of you.'

'What does it matter – as long as you do your best?' asked Mum.

'Huh – my best isn't good enough,' growled Kitty.

Now the class was practising for all the events. Kitty watched Rosie come in first in the running race, and the long jump, and the high jump, and the sack race, too. She beat all the boys. Kitty felt so pleased.

They sat cross-legged in a group around the teacher, who said, 'Now children, I want you to choose partners for the three-legged race. So when I call your name, stand up, choose your partner and line up.'

After a minute she called out Rosie's name. Kitty sat up straight, and smiled. But Rosie wasn't looking at her. 'Er . . . Tom!' she said, excitedly.

Kitty felt as if the smile was glued to her face. She wouldn't let anyone see how hurt she was. But inside she felt like a crumpled ball of paper.

'It's all right, Kitty, you can be *my* partner,' whispered William.

Tom was tall, and very good at all sports. Of course he and Rosie finished first, giggling as they jogged over the line in front of all the other pairs. Kitty and William did quite well. At least they didn't fall over.

But Kitty felt strange inside. She was sad but she was angry too. It was a funny mixture.

At lunch-time Rosie came and sat next to her as usual, and opened her lunch box.

'You're very quiet, Kitty,' she said.

'Well, what do you expect,' said Kitty, in

her crossest voice, 'when you don't want to be my friend any more?'

Rosie looked surprised, so Kitty explained. 'And you promised I would always be your partner,' she ended.

'Did I?' asked Rosie, frowning.

Kitty nodded.

'But, Kitty, the thing is, I wanted . . . oh, I wanted to *win*, you see. And because I'm taller than you . . . well, we couldn't run together. It wouldn't work.'

'And you think winning is more important than being friends?' Kitty demanded.

Rosie shook her head. 'No. They're different, that's all. You're brilliant at art, and if there was a competition where you had to do a picture with a partner, you wouldn't want *me*. I'm hopeless at it, and you know that, don't you?'

Kitty said nothing. She hadn't thought of that. Rosie offered her a crisp.

'The IMPORTANT thing is, Kit – a friend is someone you choose to *talk* to. So now will you stop being so quiet? It doesn't suit you!'

Kitty felt suddenly happy. 'OK, Rosie,' she said.

But you promised!

. . . He'd get better

William's cat was very very old. At least, he wasn't really William's cat. His parents had bought Copper before Sally was born, so he was really a family pet. But it was William who fed him. And William loved him most of all.

One day Kitty went next door to find William looking sad and worried. Copper was ill. Very ill. His orangey-brown fur wasn't sleek and shiny any more, and he just lay in his basket not wanting to do anything. He even left his favourite cat food on the plate.

'What's the matter with him?' asked Kitty.

'We don't know,' said William, 'but he's never been like this before, have you, old thing?' And he stroked Copper gently.

William and Kitty went to William's Mum, who sat with Sally in the kitchen. 'Mum, what are we going to do about Copper?' asked

107

William, and to Kitty's surprise he sounded as if he was going to cry. She didn't blame him. She felt worried, too.

'I'm sure he'll get better, Will,' said Sally.

'Of course, he will!', said their mother.

'Are you sure?' asked William.

'Of course!' said his Mum.

'Promise?' said William.

'Yes, darling.'

When Kitty heard *that* she had a funny feeling . . . but William looked more cheerful. He went to tuck an old blanket over Copper, then he and Kitty played outside.

In the morning, when Kitty and her Mum collected him to walk to school, William looked miserable again. Copper was worse.

'Don't worry, love, I'll take him to the vet today,' said his mother.

At break Kitty and William talked about Copper. At lunch-time Kitty sat with William instead of Rosie, and they wondered how he was. When it came to going-home time, Kitty's mother had to stop them both running at full speed to find out.

They ran round to William's back door and pushed it open. His Mum sat at the kitchen table, and jumped when they rushed in. Her face was pale and sad. 'MUM! How's Copp. . . ?' William began.

'Oh, William, I'm so sorry . . . it's so sad . . . I took Copper to the vet's, and . . .

and . . . he isn't alive,' said William's Mum. This time *she* sounded as if she was going to cry.

'But why. . . ?' said William, in a small voice.

'He was too ill and too old. The vet had to put him to sleep. It didn't hurt him, Will.'

William stamped his foot. 'But you promised me he'd get better, Mum! YOU PROMISED!' he shouted, and then ran out of the room, slamming the door.

Kitty started to follow him, but his mother shook her head, looking very sad. 'Leave him, Kitty,' she said.

At home, Kitty sat down in the sitting room, without saying a word. Daniel was watching television. The chattering noise irritated Kitty. Suddenly she jumped up, and switched it off. 'Hey!' protested Daniel, then stopped – because Kitty burst into tears.

Dan fetched Mum, and when Mum had put Kitty on her knee and hugged her and wiped her eyes, Kitty explained why she was upset.

'*Why* do animals have to die, Mum?' she whispered, looking across the room to where Sandy scampered around her cage.

'Because . . .'

'Because what?'

'Because they just do. And so do we. We

just live longer,' said Mum, holding Kitty
close.

'William's Mum shouldn't have made that
promise, then,' said Kitty. And she explained
what his mother had said.

'Oh, but, Kitty, remember what Dad always
says?' said Mum.

'When grown-ups say "*I promise*", they
usually mean "*I hope*",' said Kitty.

'Exactly,' said Mum.

Next day, in school, William was very quiet. At break he sat with Kitty in a corner, and they talked about Copper again. Kitty wanted him to feel better. 'You know, Will, Copper's probably having a lovely time in Heaven,' she said.

William looked at her. His eyes lit up. 'Promise me that's true!' he said.

Kitty said nothing for a few seconds. Then she smiled at him – feeling very grown-up all of a sudden – and said, 'I can't do that, Will – but let's just say, I *hope*.'

But you promised!

. . . We'd go out

It was a lovely, hot summer Saturday. Kitty and Daniel wanted to go to the park. Mum had said she would take them. She had *promised* they would go out.

But now she sat at the desk in the corner of the sitting room, doing sums on her calculator. 'I have to get this done, kids,' she said.

'Oh, WHY do grown-ups always break their promises?' said Daniel.

'Because they say "I promise" just to keep us quiet,' growled Kitty.

'Honestly, you two! You've jolly well got to understand that this is part of my new job, and I have to do it this morning,' said Mum. 'The thing about being grown-up is – things can't be all play.'

'Well I don't want to be a grown-up, I can promise you that!' muttered Kitty, cradling

Sandy in her hands and thinking it was more fun being a hamster than a child.

William's mother had arranged to take them swimming in the afternoon, and they had a marvellous time. But when they got home they heard Mum and Dad arguing.

'You just forgot!' said Mum.

'I've been really busy,' said Dad.

'But you PROMISED we'd go out!' said Mum, sounding really cross and very upset at the same time.

'I know I did,' said Dad, unhappily. 'But it's too late to get a babysitter now.'

'You forgot our anniversary last year, too,' said Mum.

'I didn't exactly forget this year . . . I just forgot to organise a babysitter,' said Dad.

'Huh. And last year you made a *solemn promise* you'd take me out for a marvellous dinner,' sniffed Mum.

Daniel looked at Kitty, and Kitty looked at Daniel. 'Quick,' she hissed. 'We've got to think of a plan.' Mum and Dad sat in the sitting room not speaking to each other. And Kitty and Daniel crept into the kitchen and whispered . . .

Twenty minutes later Kitty went to the sitting room and called them. 'Come and see what we've done!' she said.

Surprised, but still looking cross with each other, Mum and Dad got up and followed her through the kitchen into the back garden. Then they stood and stared.

Daniel had set up the garden table, and Kitty had covered it with a pretty cloth. They had set two places with the best knives and forks and china, and put a sparkling wine glass at each place.

Dan had found a dusty bottle of wine, a present from some visitors, and Kitty had picked ten fine roses, for the number of years

Mum and Dad had been married. They had lit a candle in the middle of the table (even though it was still light), and moved the radio to the kitchen windowsill, so that romantic music drifted into the garden . . .

'There you are!' said Kitty. 'Now all Dad has to do is drive down to that Greek restaurant you like and get a takeaway!'

'And we're the waiters,' added Dan.

Mum's eyes shone all bright and damp – and she ran to hug them both. Then Dad put out

an arm, and gave *her* a really huge cuddle.

'Was this your idea all along, dear?' said Mum softly, smiling at him.

'I'm not going to let myself off the hook that easily,' said Dad. 'No, it was their idea. I didn't put them up to it. I'm just lucky I've got two brilliant children!'

'It was Kit's idea really,' said Dan. 'She said that "out" could mean the garden!'

'Yes,' said Kitty wickedly. 'I just wanted to prove to you both that promises CAN be kept!'

Explain!

Kitty always used to say she didn't want to do this or that. Then there was a change – *she* wanted to do things, but the grown-ups wouldn't let her. Instead of saying, 'I don't want to!' she found herself asking, 'Why not?' Very often.

One day, for example, she asked Mum if she could walk to school on her own. 'No,' said Mum firmly.

'Why not?'

'You know why not,' smiled Mum.

'No I don't!'

Mum thought. 'Well, because you might have an accident.'

'But there's a lollipop lady!'

'Anyway, you're too young.'

'Lots of my friends go to school on their own. So why not me?'

'*Because.*' Mum wasn't smiling now.

'Because what?' asked Kitty.

'Because I said so,' said Mum, folding her arms.

'That's not a good reason,' said Kitty.

When she went to school she told William and Rosie what had happened. 'Oh, my mum always says that,' sighed Rosie.

'So does mine,' said William.

'It's not fair,' said Kitty. 'Grown-ups never think they have to explain things.'

'They wouldn't like it if we acted the same,' said Rosie.

Just then, the bell went – but Kitty had started to think. And at play-time she told William and Rosie her plan.

'Do you both think we should all be allowed to go to school on our own, instead of being treated like babies?'

'Yes,' said Rosie and William.

'And do you think grown-ups should give proper *reasons*?' Kitty asked.

They agreed.

'Well, here's what we do . . .' said Kitty.

At home that night, Mum asked Kitty when she was going to do her homework.

'Oh, I'm not going to do it,' said Kitty.

'Why ever not?' said Mum, in a surprised voice.

'Because.'

123

'Because what.'

'Oh, because I say so, that's all,' said Kitty with a grin.

'KITTY!' shouted Mum, and before Kitty had time to explain that they didn't have any homework at all, because their teacher wasn't well, she was sent upstairs to her room, for being cheeky.

Next day the three children compared notes.

'My mum stopped my pocket money,' said William glumly.

'My mum said I couldn't have the fried chicken if I couldn't be polite,' said Rosie, with a big sigh, 'and she wouldn't let me *explain*!'

'Nor would mine,' said William. 'It didn't work, Kit.'

Kitty felt guilty. She had thought that they would give the grown-ups a taste of their own medicine, and then explain and then all the mums would promise not to say 'Because I said so' each time the children asked 'Why not?', and of course they would agree to let them go to school alone . . .

But something had gone wrong.

It simply wasn't fair.

Kitty thought about this all day, and came out of school with a *very* sulky face. In fact, she walked about two metres away from her mother, and wouldn't hold her hand.

'All right, Kitty, what's all this about?' asked Mum.

Kitty explained at last.

'But why didn't you *say* you didn't actually have any homework?' asked Mum, surprised.

'Because *you* never explain,' sniffed Kitty. 'I was just copying you.'

Her mother went very quiet for a few

minutes. Then she stopped suddenly. 'All right, Kitty, I agree with you. So now let's do a little experiment. You walk home on your own. I'm going back to school to have a word with the headmistress, before she leaves. Off you go.'

Kitty was amazed, but she wasn't going to show it. She nodded and marched off down the road, feeling very bold. If she'd looked behind her she would have seen Mum stand behind the bus-shelter and watch her. She didn't go back to school at all. Then after a while, she crept along, some way behind Kitty, keeping her eyes on her all the time.

The road was long, and led past a small park – where sometimes they would go and play on the swings. Kitty wouldn't do that tonight. Not on her own. She could see other children through the railings, playing with their mothers. It looked fun.

On she marched, the road seeming much longer than it usually did. It was strange: Kitty felt so very *small* today. When she got to the zebra crossing the lollipop lady stared at her. 'On your own?' she asked.

'Yes,' said Kitty proudly.

But she felt funny – as if everyone was looking at her.

Once over the road she had to walk down two streets before she came to theirs. Few people were around. A man came towards her, with a small dog on a lead. He smiled at Kitty, but she kept her eyes on the ground. Then she saw a small group of very big boys standing on the street corner, laughing and joking. Kitty was nervous; she didn't want to walk past them.

'Hello, squirt!' one of them called. Kitty's cheeks went very red and she wanted to cry.

Once past them, she started to run. She wanted so much to be home, where it was safe. Suddenly the bushes and trees in the gardens looked as if they were hiding a mysterious

something which might jump out at her.

At last she reached her own gate and rushed inside. She sat down on the front doorstep to wait for Mum – who appeared very soon afterwards.

'Mum,' said Kitty in a small voice, 'I don't want to walk home on my own again.'

'Oh? Why not, dear?' asked Mum.

'Just *because*,' said Kitty.

'Yes . . . and you know, that's just why *I* said no in the first place, darling,' said Mum.

And they didn't have to explain any more.

You Can't Play!

Rosie and Kitty were such good friends that they often spent time together at weekends. Kitty liked Rosie's house, because it was noisy and jolly, but usually Rosie came to Kitty's, because she liked to get away from her family.

'If you had three brothers and a big sister you'd know what I mean,' said Rosie.

'But it's nice to play in a gang,' said Kitty.

'Not when you've got no choice,' said Rosie.

One Saturday morning Rosie's dad dropped her off at Kitty's house, and the two girls munched apples while they decided what to do.

Kitty's brother Daniel came into the kitchen, twirling his cricket bat. 'Anybody want to play french cricket?' he called. Kitty thought it would be fun, and looked across at her friend. But Rosie was frowning and shaking her head, and so Kitty said no.

Daniel shrugged. 'OK – I'll go up the road to Eddie's house. He and Dave will play with me.' And he went out to find his friends.

'What shall we do then, Rosie?' asked Kitty.

'Let's play . . . Snakes and Ladders,' Rosie said.

To be honest, that wasn't what Kitty felt like doing at all – but she liked Rosie so much she agreed. They had a couple of games, then went upstairs to Kitty's room and played with her toy castle and soldiers. Then they decided to clean out Sandy the hamster – which was great fun when there were two of you. They were just finishing, and had already decided to play dressing-up next, when there was a knock on the back door.

130

It was William, from next door.

'Can I play with you?' he asked.

Before Kitty could open her mouth, Rosie said, 'No.'

William looked surprised. 'Why not?' he asked.

There was a silence. Rosie looked at Kitty and Kitty looked at Rosie, and neither of them knew what to say. Then at last Rosie blurted out, 'Because . . . *you're a boy!*' And, although Kitty felt mean, she laughed.

At that William looked very hurt, and disappeared. Kitty said nothing to Rosie, and they went upstairs to play – but somehow all the fun had gone out of the morning. Soon the doorbell rang and Rosie's dad arrived to collect her.

Kitty saw nothing of William all the rest of the weekend. This was unusual, because he and his sister Sally usually played with Daniel and Kitty at least once. But it was a cold, rainy Sunday, and Kitty thought he was probably happy indoors. She hoped so.

On Monday morning Rosie's place was empty. Kitty asked the teacher where she was, and Mrs Smith said she was ill. At break-time Kitty wandered about, missing Rosie and not knowing what to do.

In a corner of the playground she found William, crouching on the ground with Tom, having races with their tiny, fast pull-back cars.

'Hello Will,' said Kitty, sitting down beside

them. 'Can I watch?'

William turned his back on Kitty. 'No, you can't,' he said coldly.

'Why not?' Kitty asked.

'Because you're a *girl*,' said William, sending his car shooting off so fast it skidded and turned over.

Kitty was furious. She snatched up his car and held it behind her back. 'What's that got to do with it?' she shouted – and then she remembered.

Then Kitty went very red, and felt terrible. Without a word she took her hand from behind her back and held out the car to William. 'I'm sorry,' she said.

He looked at her for what seemed like a long time and then mumbled, 'Oh, all right, you can have a go if you like.'

Soon afterwards they heard the bell. Walking back to the classroom Kitty asked William if he knew the saying, 'Two's company, three's a crowd.'

William said he did.

'Well, that's the only reason Rosie didn't want you to play on Saturday. It wasn't 'cos you're a boy.'

'Oh, it couldn't be,' said William.

'Why not?' asked Kitty in a serious voice.

'Because boys are best!' he joked.

'Not when Rosie's around!' laughed Kitty, so glad they were friends again.

Holiday Plans

One morning Kitty was coming downstairs when she heard Mum and Dad talking. Or rather, she heard their talking drowned by Dan's huge, loud shout, 'OH NO!'

'What's happened?' asked Kitty, rushing into the sitting room.

'Your Aunty Susan and Uncle Joe are going to rent a cottage in Cornwall for the summer holiday,' explained Dad.

'They've asked us to share it with them, and we've said yes,' added Mum.

Now it was Kitty's turn. 'OH NO!' she shouted.

'It's not fair!' Daniel groaned.

'Don't *want* to!' said Kitty.

'But why not?' sighed Mum and Dad together.

'Because we can't stand Melissa!' yelled Kitty. (She had this picture in her mind of her

135

cousin skipping around the countryside in frilly dresses, never wanting to climb trees or get dirty – she couldn't bear it.)

Kitty was telling the truth, but it made Mum angry. 'Right,' she said firmly. 'If you're going to be mean about your cousin I don't want to talk to you. We're going to Cornwall, and that's that.'

Dad sat down to read the newspaper, Mum went into the kitchen and Daniel beckoned to Kitty. She followed him into the hall.

'We didn't handle that very well, Kit,' he

whispered, looking thoughtful. 'Now listen – I think we should start again . . .'

A little while later (giving Mum the time to calm down), Daniel and Kitty called both their parents into the sitting room. 'We're going to have a family meeting,' said Kitty.

Daniel took charge. He stood in front of the fireplace and Kitty sat on the arm of the chair near him. Mum and Dad sat on the sofa, wondering what was going to happen.

'Right,' said Daniel, 'remember we all said we wanted to go on a barge holiday this summer? 'Cos Dad loves the water?'

'Er . . . yes,' said Mum.

'Remember you *promised*?' muttered Kitty – but Dan gave her a warning look and she said no more.

'We all talked about it together, didn't we?' asked Dan.

Mum and Dad nodded.

'Right. Well, we say we don't want to go to Cornwall, and you ask why not. Shall I tell you why?'

Kitty bit her lips together, to stop herself from saying the wrong thing. Dad was looking amused. 'Yes, go on, Dan, you're like someone on television!' He smiled.

'Because you didn't ask *us*, that's why. You didn't talk to us.'

'Families should do things together,' blurted Kitty.

'Including making decisions,' said Daniel.

'Right?' said Kitty, putting her hands on her hips.

'Right!' said Daniel, folding his arms. 'So I've worked out the answer to the whole problem.'

'What's that?' asked Mum.

'We hire a big boat and invite Aunty Susan, Uncle Joe and Melissa to share it with *us*,' said Daniel.

Kitty nearly fell off the chair. She looked at her brother, opened her mouth like a fish –

then closed it again, when Daniel gave her a warning look.

'We did *promise* them we'd go on a boat,' said Dad.

'And I suppose that *would* be a way out,' said Mum. 'Anyway, they'll be here in a minute, so we can ask them.'

When the doorbell rang Kitty hissed, 'Dan, what are you doing? I can't stand Meliss . . .'

'Shut up, Kit,' he whispered, giving her a sharp kick.

When Aunty Susan and Uncle Joe were sitting with coffee and biscuits, and Melissa had finished smiling snootily at Kitty's dirty dungarees, Dan said, 'Aren't you going to ask them, Mum?'

Their mother explained how they'd forgotten their promise to take the children on a river or canal holiday and how Daniel had come up with this wonderful plan of sharing a boat, instead of a cottage. 'They *so* want to be with Melissa,' she added.

Everybody looked at Melissa, who shuddered. 'Ugh,' she said, 'I don't want to go on a nasty, cold, wet boat. I can't swim. And anyway, I want to be in a pretty cottage, with roses round the door.'

And that was that.

When the visitors had gone, Kitty looked at

Daniel with admiration. 'You're the cleverest boy in the world, Dan,' she said.

'No,' he said airily, 'I just know our lovely cousin!'

Mr Tubs Goes for a Swim

The school term seemed to whizz by, and soon Kitty and Daniel were packing excitedly.

'You can't take many things on a barge,' warned Mum. But Kitty came downstairs dragging two enormous bags of toys. There was her castle, the soldiers, the garage, three boxes of paints (different colours had run out in each one), two drawing books, crayons, a pile of books, her toy dog, a sticker album, three board games, five card games and a toy picnic set. Oh, and (of course) Mr Tubs, her favourite bear.

'Is all that necessary, Kit?' asked Dad.

Kitty nodded.

'Sorry, love, you'll have to make choices,' said Mum firmly, 'and only take what you really need. After all, we're only away for ten days.'

So it was that Kitty arrived on the barge

carrying a drawing book, crayons, two card games, some books, and Mr Tubs – because she couldn't ever sleep without him.

They loved the barge because it was just like a little house inside. Kitty raced around exploring – opening cupboards, choosing her bed, and admiring the neat little stove in the galley-kitchen. She decided right away that she must copy the pretty painted designs on the outside.

Soon it was time to set off, but first Dad

said, 'Now listen, gang, we're on a canal, and so there have to be certain rules . . .' Kitty heard his voice in the distance – but she wasn't listening. She was thinking what fun it would be to live on a barge like this always.

For two days, or maybe three, everything was perfect. The weather was wonderful, the days seemed exciting – and Kitty was very good.

Then came a chilly, rainy day, and Mum told Kitty not to go up on deck. 'Why not?' she protested, grabbing her mac and starting for the steps.

'Because it's pouring down.'

'Daniel's outside.'

'Dan's helping Dad,' said Mum.

'He's always got something to do,' said Kitty, sulkily.

Soon the sun shone again, and Kitty picked up Mr Tubs and wandered out on to the deck. She made her way up to the front of the barge. The light danced on the water, and gleamed on the damp trees – but Kitty didn't notice. She still felt cross.

'I wish you were the captain, Mr Tubs,' she whispered into her bear's furry neck. 'Then nobody would be allowed to give *me* orders.'

She placed Mr Tubs on top of the cabin roof, so that he could *look* as if he were in

charge. Just then Dad, who was standing some way away at the back of the barge, glanced up and saw her.

'Hey, don't do that, Kit,' he called. Kitty pretended not to hear. They were always telling her what to do!

'KITTY!' Dad shouted, so that it was impossible for her not to hear. 'I said don't put anything on the roof!'

Kitty glared at him and tossed her head. 'WHY NOT?' she yelled, then folded her arms, and sat down – staring hard at the canal tow-path.

It was a pity she didn't look at the water instead. For just at that moment another barge passed them, going the opposite way. It was bigger and it was faster, and the people on it waved cheerfully.

As it moved through the water it set up large waves behind it, making them rock violently from side to side. Dimly Kitty remembered Dad saying something about that on their first day, and about not leaving anything on the roof . . .

Quickly she jumped up – in time to see Mr Tubs rock, then topple over and slowly roll down the side of the roof and into the water.

Horror! Kitty screamed and started to cry.

For a few seconds she did not dare to open her eyes. She felt helpless. But then she heard shouts – and laughter. At last she forced herself to look.

Dad was standing smiling at her – and holding a dripping teddy bear high in the air. Luckily he had seen what had happened, had quickly leaned over the low side of the barge and grabbed Mr Tubs before he sank.

'Isn't it about time you taught your bear to swim?' smiled Dad.

'Two more seconds, Kit, and his fur would have been water-logged,' said Daniel, in his 'you've-learned-a-lesson' voice.

For once Kitty didn't mind. She took Mr Tubs and helped Dad shake and pummel some of the water out of him, then laid him gently on a towel, in a safe and sheltered part of the boat, to dry in the sun.

Then she went to Dad and put her hand in his. 'Dad,' she said, 'can I make you a promise?'

'Of course, Kitty-kat, what is it?'

'I promise you I'll never ask *why not* again!'

Dad put his arm round her, gave her a huge hug and whispered, 'Now don't you think you should be careful – of making promises you can't possibly keep?'

Trick or Treat?

In the days before Hallowe'en all the shops were full of witch hats, rubber spiders, plastic skeletons, masks, and lots of other spooky toys and decorations. Kitty loved them. Something thrilling was in the air – and she wanted to take part.

Their classroom was decorated with cut-out witches and broomsticks, and Mrs Smith told them lots of legends and customs about Hallowe'en.

'Are you going out trick-or-treating tomorrow night?' asked Rosie, when break-time came.

Kitty said she wasn't sure.

'I am. There's three of us in our road and we always go out together. We dress up, knock on lots of doors and get sweets and biscuits. You can come if you like.'

Kitty jumped up and down with excitement.

'Oh, thank you, Rosie, I'd love to. It'll be the best Hallowe'en ever.'

That night she was collected by William and his mum, and as soon as she reached home Kitty rushed into the sitting room and told her mother about the plan.

'Oh,' said Mum – in that voice Kitty knew well. It meant, 'You-aren't-going-to-like-what-I'm-going-to-say.'

'Well? Won't it be fun?' demanded Kitty.

'Darling, you can't go trick-or-treating,' said Mum.

'WHY NOT?'

'Because . . .' Kitty looked at her, and

waited. 'Yes, I know I've got to explain. Well, if you go and knock on people's doors . . . er . . . you might frighten old ladies.'

'Mum! That's a *silly* reason. Rosie said . . .'

'I don't care what Rosie said; *I* say you can't go.'

'But *why not*?' wailed Kitty again – looking really unhappy, as well as angry.

Mum was quiet for a few minutes. Then she took hold of Kitty's arm, and pulled her on to her lap.

'Come on, let's have a little talk. Shall I tell you the truth?'

Kitty nodded.

Mum took a deep breath. 'This isn't easy, Kitty – the truth is, I don't want you wandering the streets in the dark.'

'But I'd be with the others,' protested Kitty.

'Yes, but you might get separated from them. Children can be silly when they're excited. And you know, darling, real people can be much worse than imaginary witches, you know. You don't know *who* is wandering about the town at night – and so I won't let you go out. It's because I love you. Don't you see?'

'Couldn't the three of *us* go out, you, me, and Daniel?' pleaded Kitty.

Mum shook her head. Kitty jumped up and sighed. 'Well, I'll have to tell the others that

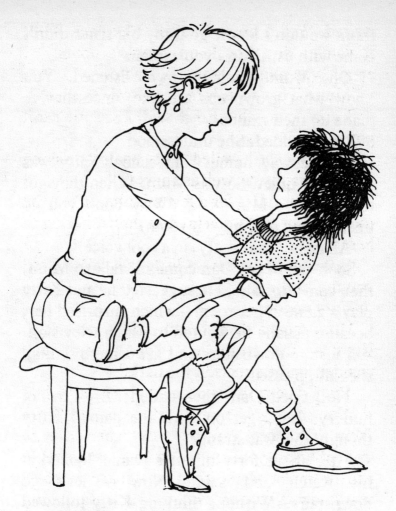

my Hallowe'en will be the most *boring* ever!
Thanks a lot, Mum!' And she ran out of the
room, leaving her mother sitting in the chair,
looking a bit sad and thoughtful.

Next day she told Rosie what had happened.
Her friend shrugged. 'Well, I suppose my

mum wouldn't let me go if my big sister didn't come with us. Didn't you explain?'

'Oh, Mum wouldn't have listened. You know what grown-ups are like, once they've made up their minds . . .'

Rosie nodded. She understood.

On the way home from school Kitty was unusually quiet. So was Mum. When they got to the house Mum said, 'Why don't you go upstairs and play in your room?'

'All right,' said Kitty, in a cool voice.

Soon she heard Dan come in, talk to Mum, then come upstairs. He suggested he and Kitty play a game in her room – which surprised her, because usually he wanted to watch television. 'I'll just go downstairs and get some biscuits,' she said, pleased.

'No!' cried Dan, then added, 'Er, I'm not hungry. Let's get on with the game.' Kitty thought that was strange.

After about forty minutes Daniel looked at his watch and said, 'Now – let's go downstairs.' Without thinking Kitty followed him. The hall lights were off, but a candle flickered on the table at the bottom of the stairs. Now that was *very* strange.

'Don't be scared, Kit,' whispered Dan, with an odd smile.

They pushed open the kitchen door . . . and

Kitty got a shock. The room was dark, lit only by a few candles. A huge orange pumpkin head grinned and glowed in the middle of the table – which was covered with a black cloth. On a chair sat . . . a ghost: a small, white lumpy shape, with round black eyes.

As Kitty moved forward nervously, something fine and tickly brushed across her face, so that she jumped back with a yelp. *Cobwebs*.

And there, by the stove, stirring a huge pot, was a tall figure, wearing a pointed hat and a black cloak. It turned and Kitty saw that her face was all white, marked with heavy black lines and spots, and surrounded by thick grey hair. 'Welcome to the witch's kitchen, little girl,' she cackled.

Now, in her *mind* Kitty knew it was Mum. But in her *heart* she believed this was a real witch and she felt rather nervous! The witch dipped her spoon into the pot and pulled out a horrible wriggling snake. Then she made Kitty touch the enormous black furry spider that sat on the table, and as she reached out it jumped – making Kitty jump too.

'Now, little girl, if you want to escape from my kitchen, you and your brother must duck for apples. If you don't bite an apple, you're my prisoner forever!' And she shrieked with cackling laughter again.

Kitty's mind thought, 'Mum's a good actress.' But her heart thought, 'Help!'

The witch brought out a large bowl of water, on which some apples bobbed – and Kitty and

Daniel got wet faces and hair trying to grab them with their mouths. It was such fun.

Then the witch gave them dried insects to eat (which looked very like crisps) and blood to drink (which tasted just like blackcurrant juice).

Suddenly the light snapped on and there was Dad.

'What's going on?' he began, staring at his dripping children. Then he looked at Mum, and laughed.

They showed him the jumpy plastic spider and the rubber snake, then pulled the sheet off the funny, lumpy little ghost – who turned out to be Mr Tubs. The 'cobwebs' were long pieces of black cotton, pinned up on the door frame.

'It was a trick *and* a treat, Dad,' said Kitty.

At last Mum pulled off her hat, with the long woollen hair attached – she still looked funny, with her ugly make-up – and Kitty ran and threw her arms around her.

'I don't want you to stop being a witch,' she whispered.

'Why not?' smiled Mum.

'Because now I know that witches are the nicest, kindest people in the world,' said Kitty.

The Visit

Gran was in hospital. Mum and Dad looked worried most of the time and went to see her often. Kitty painted her a beautiful get-well card and took it to show Mum.

'I'll take it to her this afternoon – when you go,' Kitty said.

'It's really beautiful, love, and it'll make her feel better – but you can't come and visit,' said Mum.

'Why not?' asked Kitty – of course.

'Because . . . because Gran's *very* ill this time,' said Mum, looking serious. Then Kitty felt very sad.

'But she will get better, won't she, Mum? You've got to tell me the truth – because I'm older now.'

Mum didn't speak at first. She seemed to be thinking hard. Then she sat down at the kitchen table, and sighed. 'No, Kitty, I don't

think she will get better.'

'But *why not*?' wailed Kitty.

'Because she's got something the matter with her which the doctors aren't sure how to cure. And Gran is very old, you see, so it makes it harder . . .'

'Oh,' said Kitty. She didn't know what else to say.

In her own room, she thought and thought. She looked at all her toys, her bed with its patterned duvet, all the cuddly animals on their shelf and the posters on the walls – all the things she most liked. And she decided that she'd happily give them all away if only Gran could get better.

After a while Dad came in to talk to her, and she told him how she felt.

'Dad – I don't want you and Mum to get old.'

He smiled. 'I was going to ask "why not?", like you always do, but I know why not. We never want people we love to change. The thing is, Kit, *everybody* has to grow old.'

Kitty shivered. 'But it's so sad! Oh, why can't we always stay the same forever, you and Mum, me and Dan – and Gran?'

Dad put out his arm and hugged her. He was smiling very gently. 'Because we can't, Kit – and that's a fact. Look, even Sandy the hamster is getting older. And the trees . . . everything! Even your old dad. And *that's* why we mustn't waste precious time being miserable. Now, how do you fancy a choc ice?'

A few days went by, and Mum and Dad looked more worried than ever. They went to the hospital a lot, and the phone rang, and Aunty Susan came round . . . and Kitty knew that Gran had had a big operation. It was scary.

She and Dan talked and wished they knew what was going on. But they had to go to school and get on with things – Mum said.

But, *'What if Gran dies?'* whispered Kitty.

Then one afternoon William's mum brought her home from school and she ran into the house – to find Mum with her coat on, looking like someone with a secret. Dad came in with Daniel and asked, 'Are we all ready?'

'Where are we going?' asked Kitty.

'It's a surprise,' said Mum.

Kitty recognised the way they were going. It led to the hospital. She felt very nervous and wanted to ask questions, but didn't dare.

They walked along corridors which smelt funny, past nurses and doctors, and Kitty felt even more afraid. But Mum and Dad held her hands and Daniel looked so cheerful . . .

At last they reached the ward – there, sitting up in bed, looking a bit pale, but lovely with

her hair in a bun, was Gran. She wore a frilly bed-jacket.

Flowers and cards surrounded her, with Kitty's card right in the middle. Gran was smiling widely and held out her arms to Kitty – who would have jumped on the bed, only it was too high.

'Be gentle, Kitty,' said Mum, 'Gran's had a bad time.'

'Oh, but I'm better now,' said Gran, holding Dan's hand one side of the bed and Kitty's the other. 'I'm much tougher than everybody thinks, you know!'

Then she gave Daniel and Kitty big bars of chocolate she had bought from the hospital trolley. Mum took out packets of biscuits and drinks for the children, and a nurse brought the grown-ups some tea.

'This is Gran's get-well party, isn't it?' said Kitty happily.

'Oh no,' said Gran, 'I wouldn't want a get-well party.'

'Why not?' asked Kitty.

'Because I AM well!' laughed Gran.

Kitty's Great Idea

Kitty was watching television one evening when she had a great idea. The programme was about nature and how it was really important to leave old hedges alone so that wild flowers could grow, and small animals and insects make their homes.

Now Kitty's parents believed in letting nature have its own way. They didn't use any artificial things to make the grass grow, or kill weeds. 'Weeds can be so pretty,' said Kitty's mum. 'In the country they're called wild flowers!'

So their garden was wild and the hedge that ran along the bottom was huge and tangly. It was easy to imagine whole families of mice having a little city there, just like in the picture books. They were all proud of that hedge.

But the man who lived behind their house (so that the hedge was between their gardens), kept complaining about it. His garden was really neat. He said the hedge was too high and too messy and Kitty's dad got very angry because Mr Simpson tried to make it thinner.

'Oh, dear, it's terrible quarrelling with neighbours,' said Kitty's mum. 'If only people could see that nature *matters*.'

So Kitty had her great idea.

'Mum,' she said, 'why don't we open our garden so people can come and see it? Like in those posh houses? We can have a collection, for a nature charity or something. And we could invite that man we saw on TV – the one in the government who's in charge of the in . . . in . . .'

'Environment,' said Daniel, with a grin.

164

'Don't be so stupid, Kitty, that would *never* work!'

'Why not?' said Kitty.

'Because, darling, it's a sweet, but impossible idea,' smiled Mum.

Kitty folded her arms. This was a challenge. 'All right then, what's the name of that man?'

'Mr Thornton – Christopher Thornton,' said Mum. 'But really, Kitty . . .'

Kitty didn't wait to hear the rest. She went up into her bedroom and got out the new box of rainbow-coloured stationery she had been given for her birthday. Then, very, very carefully, in her best handwriting, she wrote two letters – setting them out just as they had been shown in school.

First she wrote to the local paper and told them that her family had a wild garden with a beautiful hedge and lots of butterflies – and because everybody had to be interested in the environment (she had to look that up in her dictionary) she would be opening the garden to the public on Saturday 20 April.

Then she wrote to Christopher Thornton, telling him the same thing and asking him to come along and see. She didn't quite know where to send this letter, so this was how she addressed it:

Mr Christopher Thornton, MP.
The Man in Charge of the Environment,
The Government,
House of Parliament, LONDON.

She went and asked for two stamps, and frowned because Mum and Dad were still laughing at her.

'They'll never write back to you,' said Daniel.

'Why not?'

'Because you're only a little girl,' he replied.

'You'll see,' she muttered.

A week passed, and nothing happened. Every morning Kitty looked for letters, but none came. 20 April was five days away. She felt very disappointed.

Then, on Monday morning, Dad came into breakfast waving an envelope. It was typed and addressed to Kitty. They all watched as she opened it. This is what it said:

Dear Kitty,
Thank you for your lovely letter.
It is very nice to know that children like
you are so interested in nature. I like
wild gardens too.
As it happens I have to make a speech in
a town very near yours on Saturday night.
So I could come along on the way and see
your lovely garden and wonderful old hedge.
We should be there at about three o'clock
and look forward to meeting you
and your parents.

Your sincerely,
Christopher Thornton
(The Man in Charge of the Environment)

Kitty thought Mum would faint. Dad sat down heavily and gasped, 'Well, who would have thought . . .?' And Kitty just stuck out her tongue at Daniel and said, '*See!*'

That night the telephone rang and the local paper asked if they could come and take a photograph of Kitty by the hedge. When Dad

told them that Christopher Thornton was coming to visit they got very excited and said they'd write about that too. On the Friday there was a picture of Kitty – with a short article saying she was opening their garden in aid of a charity which tried to save the environment – and that she had actually got Mr Thornton to come.

Saturday 20 April was a beautiful clear day. Kitty and Daniel set up a table by the gate, and waited. Sure enough, people started to arrive, each one putting 15p into a box. They'd all seen the newspaper. By the time it came to the afternoon there was quite a crowd.

Just before three o'clock lots of

photographers arrived, and when the sleek black car pulled up at their gate there was such a noise of clicking and such a buzz of excitement Kitty felt quite afraid. But Christopher Thornton beamed at her and shook her hand in front of all the cameras. When Kitty told him he had to put his money in the box everybody roared with laughter – she didn't know why.

It was like a dream. Kitty showed Mr Thornton, and the people with him, all around the garden and they spent a long time admiring the hedge and talking with Dad about things called pesticides and weed-killers which did harm.

Then Mum gave them tea (using her best china, of course) and it was time to go. But before he left, Christopher Thornton hugged

Kitty, saying she reminded him of his own little girl and he gave her a lovely book about wild-life.

As they went down the front path to say goodbye, Kitty noticed bad-tempered Mr Simpson, from the house behind, standing by the front gate and staring so hard she thought his eyes would fall out of his head.

Dad didn't miss the chance. With a twinkle

in his eye he introduced Mr Thornton, saying, 'This is another of our neighbours. The hedge borders his garden too.'

'Does it? Well, I think you're very lucky,' smiled Christopher Thornton, shaking Mr Simpson's hand.

'Er . . . thank you . . . er . . . oh yes, I know. Nice to meet you,' stuttered their neighbour – pink with pleasure at meeting someone so important.

And then Kitty knew that her great idea – the one they'd called impossible – had worked, even beyond her wildest dreams. For they wouldn't have any trouble with Mr Simpson again!

The Puzzle

Kitty was bored. She couldn't go to William's house because he had 'flu, and when she rang Rosie to see if she could come over to play, there was no reply. And it was pouring with rain.

'Will you play a game with me, Daniel?' Kitty asked, wandering into his room.

'No, Kit,' he said, hunched over his desk.

'Why not?'

'Because I want to finish this model aeroplane and it's really fiddly,' he said, without even looking up.

So Kitty went downstairs to find Dad. He wasn't in the sitting room, but Kitty heard the clatter of plates and found him in the kitchen, washing the breakfast things.

'Dad – shall we have a game of Monopoly? You know it's your favourite and you always win . . .' asked Kitty, in a wheedling voice.

'Sorry, Kit,' said Dad, wiping his hands.

'Why not?' she asked, feeling disappointed, because Dad was usually such fun.

'Because I've got to finish this and it's my turn to cook lunch today, so I'm going to do that next – it's a dish that needs a long time in the oven.'

'Boring!' said Kitty.

'You'd say that if there was no lunch,' grinned Dad.

Then Kitty went in search of Mum and found her at the desk in the sitting room.

'Mum,' said Kitty, 'will you *do* something with me?'

'I'm sorry, my love . . .' said Mum in that voice Kitty hated – all far away, as if she hadn't really heard at all.

'Why *not*?' said Kitty. She felt very sulky now.

'Because I've got to do this work, ready for my job on Monday,' said Mum, her fingers tapping the calculator as she spoke. 'Honestly, Kit, surely you're old enough to be able to play on your own.'

Kitty went upstairs and sat down at her own desk. It was so boring, she thought, that people always said 'No' to things, instead of trying to work out how they could happen . . .

Something made her take a piece of plain paper and write 'WHY NOT' and then 'SEE HOW'. She looked at those four words for quite a while, drawing boxes around them and wondering what to do. 'How to change the "why not" into the "see how" . . .' she murmured, staring at the words and starting to think.

She had found something to do. It took quite a while, but Kitty had great fun working it out. At last she took three clean sheets of paper, wrote out her puzzle on each one and ran downstairs.

First she went into the sitting room. She knew Mum could never resist a challenge. 'Here you are, Mum,' she said. 'I've worked out a puzzle for you. Bet you can't do it!'

'Oh, you do, do you? Let's see,' said Mum.

This was on the paper:

WHY NOT

· · · · · ·

· · · · · ·

· · · · · ·

· · · · · ·

SEE HOW

'You've got to change "why not" into "see how", changing only one letter each time, on each whole line,' Kitty explained. 'But one letter stays the same all the way.'

'This should be easy,' said Mum.

Just then Dad came into the room. 'What's going on?' he asked. Kitty explained. Mum was too busy staring at the puzzle and doodling with her pencil on a spare bit of paper to say anything.

'Bet you can't beat Mum,' smiled Kitty.

'Oh yes?' said Dad. He put down his wooden spoon on Mum's papers, grabbed a pencil and sat down in a chair.

Kitty ran upstairs and told Daniel there was a competition. He put down his glue like a shot and ran downstairs.

'Should be easy,' he said, 'once you know the "o" stays the same.'

'Well, *try*,' said Kitty.

'Sshh,' said Mum and Dad together.

Some time later, Mum laughed, and said she'd got it. Dad put down his pencil and groaned. Daniel asked Kitty for the answer. (But see if you can do it, before you look.)

'Easy,' she said. 'This is how it goes . . .'

WHY NOT
WHY NOW
SHY NOW
SHE NOW
SEE NOW
SEE HOW

Mum and Dad smiled and Dad said, 'Is there a message in this, Kit-Kat?'

Kitty nodded. 'Yes, instead of thinking of reasons *not* to do things, why not try to see how we *can* do things?'

'Ahah!' said Dad.

'Well, I won,' said Mum, 'so what's my prize?'

'A family game of Monopoly,' said Kitty. 'And before you all say "No", I've worked out how. You all do what you're doing for twenty more minutes and *then* we play.'

'That, Kitty,' said Dad, 'is what grown-ups call a compromise.'

'And it proves our girl is growing up,' said Mum, ruffling Kitty's hair.

'No I'm not,' said Kitty.

'Why not?' asked Mum.

'Because when you're grown-up you don't want to play games,' said Kitty.

'Oh yes, we do,' roared Dad, 'in fact – we'll play NOW!'

Also by Bel Mooney

I DON'T WANT TO!

Kitty's favourite word is NO! She doesn't want to clean her teeth or wash or eat her vegetables or – worst of all – play with boring cousin Melissa. But saying no gives Kitty more problems than even *she* bargained for – and somehow she always ends up wanting to say yes!

I CAN'T FIND IT!

Kitty was always losing things. She wasn't care-less, but things she put away very, very carefully just – sort of – moved, all by themselves . . . Then one day, Kitty finds something no one else can find.

This is the hilarious and touching sequel to I DON'T WANT TO!

Tony Bradman

DILLY THE DINOSAUR

Dilly is the naughtiest dinosaur in the whole world.

There was the time he decided he wasn't ever going to wash again. Another day he decorated his bedroom using his sister's best painting set.

And when he *doesn't* get his way, he opens his mouth and lets loose his ultra-special, 150-mile-per-hour super-scream!

Other DILLY titles are

Dilly's Muddy Day
Dilly Tells the Truth
Dilly & the Worst Day Ever
Dilly & the Tiger
Dilly & the Ghost
Dilly Dinosaur, Superstar
Dilly the Angel

Anne Fine

A SUDDEN PUFF OF GLITTERING SMOKE

'"Not G-e-n-i-e! J-e-a-n-i-e!"
The creature shrugged. "One little mistake," he said. "Even a genie gets rusty after five hundred years stuck in a ring." '

The disgruntled genie who appears on her desk seems to be the answer to Jeanie's problems – whatever she wishes, he will command. But Jeanie quickly discovers that she and her genie have very different views of the world.

A Sudden Puff of Glittering Smoke is the first part in Anne Fine's trilogy about a genie; followed by *A Sudden Swirl of Icy Wind*, the trilogy is concluded in *A Sudden Glow of Gold*.

Anne Fine is the winner of the Smarties Award (for *Bill's New Frock*) and the Carnegie Medal.

Dorothy Edwards

MY NAUGHTY LITTLE SISTER

Dorothy Edwards' well-known collections of stories about Naughty Little Sister are loved by children everywhere – just right for reading aloud at bedtime or anytime.

Also available

More Naughty Little Sister Stories
My Naughty Little Sister and Bad Harry
My Naughty Little Sister's Friends
When My Naughty Little Sister Was Good

Jill Tomlinson

THE AARDVARK WHO
WASN'T SURE

Pim is a baby aardvark. His mother has told him
so. But Pim still isn't quite sure, because he
doesn't seem to be able to do any of the things
that other aardvarks can do. As he grows up,
however, Pim finds out that these things have to
be learned, sometimes from his mother and sometimes from the other creatures he meets. As time
goes on, he becomes increasingly sure that he
really *is* an aardvark after all!

Also by Jill Tomlinson

The Cat Who Wanted to Go Home
The Gorilla Who Wanted to Grow Up
The Hen Who Wouldn't Give Up
The Otter Who Wanted to Know
The Owl Who Was Afraid of the Dark
Penguin's Progress

Margaret Greaves

CHARLIE, EMMA AND ALBERIC

Charlie and Emma want a pet of their own. Then one day they find a tiny dragon. Of course, Alberic wants to go home with them – and that's when their adventures start!

The first story of Charlie, Emma and their magic dragon.

Also available

Charlie, Emma and the Dragon Family
Charlie, Emma and the School Dragon
Charlie, Emma and Dragons to the Rescue
Charlie, Emma and the Juggling Dragon

Jeff Brown

FLAT STANLEY

Stanley Lambchop is just a normal healthy boy, though since a large notice-board fell on him, he's been only half an inch thick!

For Stanley this presents no problems, in fact he finds he can do all sorts of things and go to places never before possible.

Jeff Brown's hilarious text and Tomi Ungerer's equally funny drawings make this book absolutely irresistible.

The adventures of the Lambchop family continue in *Stanley and the Magic Lamp* and *Stanley in Space*.

A selected list of titles available from Mammoth

While every effort is made to keep prices low, it is sometimes necessary to increase prices at short notice. Mandarin Paperbacks reserves the right to show new retail prices on covers which may differ from those previously advertised in the text or elsewhere.

The prices shown below were correct at the time of going to press.

☐ 7497 0366 0	**Dilly the Dinosaur**	Tony Bradman	£2.50
☐ 7497 0137 4	**Flat Stanley**	Jeff Brown	£2.50
☐ 7497 0306 7	**The Chocolate Touch**	P Skene Catling	£2.50
☐ 7497 0568 X	**Dorrie and the Goblin**	Patricia Coombs	£2.50
☐ 7497 0114 5	**Dear Grumble**	W J Corbett	£2.50
☐ 7497 0054 8	**My Naughty Little Sister**	Dorothy Edwards	£2.50
☐ 7497 0723 2	**The Little Prince (colour ed.)**	A Saint-Exupery	£3.99
☐ 7497 0305 9	**Bill's New Frock**	Anne Fine	£2.99
☐ 7497 0590 6	**Wild Robert**	Diana Wynne Jones	£2.50
☐ 7497 0661 9	**The Six Bullerby Children**	Astrid Lindgren	£2.50
☐ 7497 0319 9	**Dr Monsoon Taggert's Amazing Finishing Academy**	Andrew Matthews	£2.50
☐ 7497 0420 9	**I Don't Want To!**	Bel Mooney	£2.50
☐ 7497 0833 6	**Melanie and the Night Animal**	Gillian Rubinstein	£2.50
☐ 7497 0264 8	**Akimbo and the Elephants**	A McCall Smith	£2.50
☐ 7497 0048 3	**Friends and Brothers**	Dick King-Smith	£2.50
☐ 7497 0795 X	**Owl Who Was Afraid of the Dark**	Jill Tomlinson	£2.99

All these books are available at your bookshop or newsagent, or can be ordered direct from the publisher. Just tick the titles you want and fill in the form below.

Mandarin Paperbacks, Cash Sales Department, PO Box 11, Falmouth, Cornwall TR10 9EN.

Please send cheque or postal order, no currency, for purchase price quoted and allow the following for postage and packing:

UK including BFPO — £1.00 for the first book, 50p for the second and 30p for each additional book ordered to a maximum charge of £3.00.

Overseas including Eire — £2 for the first book, £1.00 for the second and 50p for each additional book thereafter.

NAME (Block letters) ....

ADDRESS ....

....

☐ I enclose my remittance for ....

☐ I wish to pay by Access/Visa Card Number ☐☐☐☐☐☐☐☐☐☐☐☐☐☐☐☐

Expiry Date ☐☐☐☐